Learning the History of Kelley Park in San Jose

Paul Trainer
Edited by Leonard McKay

www.trafford.com
North America & international
toll-free: 1 888 232 4444 (USA & Canada)
fax: 812 355 4082

Learning the History of Kelley Park in San Jose

The Lord walks not only in front and behind me.
He rises above and watches where he leads me.
Paul Trainer

Sometimes when I look at my son I see him struggling,
trying and wanting to become a man and I also see
his sadness knowing he will never be a child again.
Paul Trainer

This is the first book of its kind to be written with special
places of family interest and these animated characters.
This book is dedicated to teachers, students, children, hospitals,
institutions, educational programs, care centers, libraries,
historians, schools, bookstores and non-profit organizations.

✝ **And to My Father**
Paul Arthur Trainer
A Man who loved his Wife and Family
Oct. 3, 1920—Aug. 26, 2005
A New Life Begins

Books order information at
www. prtproductions.com

Special thanks to Leonard McKay for his expertise
on not only writing, but for his approval of this book.

Happy Hollow

Archer House

Japanese Friendship
Gardens

History Park

Lawrence Archer was a San Jose lawyer and twice mayor of the city

The original Archer home burned in 1909. After the house was rebuilt, Louise Archer Flavin Kelley, left, lived in it for 40 years.

*Leininger Center San Jose Parks reservation center

San Jose Mercury News ■ September 29, 1982

Thirty-one years ago, the city of San Jose acquired 63 acres of a country estate on the west bank of the Coyote Creek. City officials called it Kelly Park after the woman who sold it to the city. And they put in a zoo, a children's play area, a community-center building, the Japanese Friendship Garden, a historical museum, picnic areas and train rides. Today it is the subject of controversy. Marine World-Africa USA likes the looks of the parcel on the east side of Coyote Creek off Senter Road and Capitol Expressway. Residents in the area like the park the way it is - peaceful and without the baying of lions and honking traffic. Few know the history of the place they call Kelley Park. When it was sold for $142,000, it was going to be named Archer Park. Louise Archer Flavin Kelley hoped that it would be called after her maiden name. Instead, the city chose to name it Kelley. In an interview in August 1951. Mrs Kelley, then 88, told me her father bought the original 160 acres in 1861 and moved the family from its large residence at Fountain and Second streets in 1869. She was then 6 years old. In 1951, she had lived in the home for 40 consecutive years, working in the extensive gardens and devoting her energies to landscaping and improving the estate. She was the daughter of Lawrence Archer, distinguished San Jose lawyer, twice mayor of the city, one-time county judge and member of the state legislature.

Archer, a native of South Carolina, practiced law in Mississippi. In 1843, he became the pioneer lawyer in the new little frontier community of St. Joseph on the Missouri River. The next year, he was elected district attorney, serving until May 1852, when he joined a wagon train bound for California. He settled in San Jose in January 1853 and almost immediately became involved in the city's affairs. He was elected mayor in 1856 and again in 1878; served as county judge from 1868 to 1871; was a member of the state assembly in 1875; member of the first Board of Regents of the University of California; and a member of the state Board of Normal School Trustees. The Archer building stood at 32 S. Second St. for many years and was finally torn down to make room for a parking lot. Judge Archer had his law offices in another building he owned at First and Santa Clara streets, according to Mrs. Kelley, who also remembered that the town pump was at First and Fountain (formerly known as Archer Alley) streets. Judge Archer called his country estate (in Kelley Park) Lone Oak, and in later years when his daughter made her home there, it was called Arc-Kel Villa for the Archer-Kelly families. The judge planted 40 acres in cherries and other fruits and landscaped the acres around the two-story home. The house in which the judge died and in which Mrs. Kelly lived for 40 years is used for storage, ranger offices and recreation programs. This house replaced the original, which burned in May 1909. The new house had only been completed one day when judge Archer died Feb. 17, 1910. He was the father of three children. Mrs. Kelley was a daughter by his first wife, and Lawrence and Leo (the latter a prominent San Jose attorney) were sons by his second wife. Little Miss Archer grew up in San Jose and graduated from the old San Jose Normal School with the class of 1881.

Two years later, she married Martin J. Flavin, a San Francisco businessman, in an elaborate wedding held in the Archer home. The wedding filled more than two columns on page 1 of The San Jose Daily Mercury, the lists of guests taking up more than half the space. The society reporter pulled out all the stops in describing both the bride and groom, as well as the beauty of the setting with an abundance of punctuation marks. Flavin died a few years later, and Louise Archer Flavin married Frank J. Kelley, founder of the Star-Peerless Wallpaper Mills in Chicago Ill.

The couple went to Chicago to live, but on the death of her father, Mrs. Kelly returned to make her home permanently on the country estate. She was the mother of four sons, Frank J. Kelley Jr.; Dr. Kenneth Kelley, Lawrence A Kelley; and Martin Flavin, Pulitzer Prize-winning author. Mrs. Kelly sold the estate to two San Jose public-spirited businessmen, Ernest H. Renzel and Alden Campen, who agreed to act as the city's agents at no cost to the city.

*San Jose Mercury News Clipping

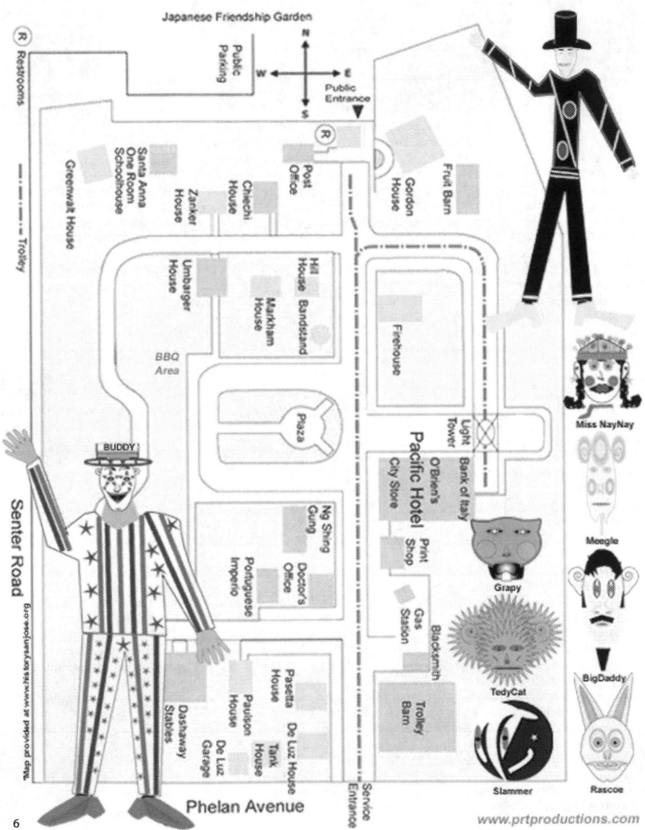

Japanese Friendship Garden

Public Parking

N
W — E
S

Public Entrance

R Restrooms
Trolley

Greenwalt House
Santa Ana One Room Schoolhouse
Zanker House
Chiechi House
Post Office

Umbarger House
Markham House
Hill House
Bandstand

BBQ Area

Plaza

Ng Shing Gung
Portuguese Imperio
Doctor's Office

Pasetta House
Pavlion House
Dashaway Stables
De Luz House
De Luz Garage
Tank House

Senter Road

www.prtproductions.com

Phelan Avenue

Service Entrance

Gordon House
Fruit Barn

Firehouse

Light Tower
Bank of Italy
O'Brien's City Store
Pacific Hotel
Print Shop

Gas Station
Blacksmith
Trolley Barn

BUDDY

Miss NayNay

Maggie

Grapy

BigDaddy

TedyCat

Slammer

Rascoe

6

Hello everyone and welcome. My name is Buddy and this is my friend Mr. Disbig. The History Park is located at the south end of Kelly Park, then you have the Japanese Friendship Garden in the center, and at the north end you have Happy Hollow. These three parks are different from each other, and yet, very special in their own way. Along with a few of our friends, you will be receiving a fantasic tour around these parks. We will begin with History San Jose, also known as HSJ. I would like to bring your attention to the map. Now if any kids are helping your parents read, maybe you could tell them what directions to take. We will be starting at the South (back) Gate, which is the service entrance, then moving West up to the North (main) Gate and coming back around toward the East. We will eventually end up back where we started. But first, let me tell you a little about how the History Park was started.

1963 - Museum concept adopted by Historic Landmarks Commission

1964 - Historic Landmarks Commission visits Kern County's Museum's Pioneer "Village" type Museum. Council turns down request on advice from Director of Parks and Recreation, Planning Commission, and City Manager.

1965 - Historic Landmarks Commission with help from Department of Public Works (Architectural Engineering) lays out a proposed town site at Kelly Park. First attempt by Historic Landmarks Commission to have a Museum Director position put into the city's budget. Unsuccessful.

1966 - Historic Landmarks Commission compiles a list of buildings that would be suitable to move into proposed historical town site. Second attempt by Historic Landmarks Commission to have a museum Director put into the city's budget. Unsuccessful.

1967 - City buys Bohnett Collection of antique autos, motorcycles, animal-drawn carriages, amusement machines, dolls, dishes, clothes, etc... from Trader Lew Bohnett for $235,000. Mr. Theron Fox, Landmarks President, made the deal for the city. Mr. Earnest Renzel put up the cash for the collection and the city paid Mr. Renzel $50,000 per year. Third attempt by Historic Landmarks Commission to have a museum Director put into the city's budget. Unsuccessful.

1968 - City builds two steel warehouses to take care of Bohnett Collection and other artifacts for future Museum. Forth attempt by Historic Landmarks Commission to have a museum Director put into the city's budget. Unsuccessful.

1969 - Museum Directors position approved for 1969-1970 budget. Mr. John B. Dowty appointed Director in September of 1969. Plans begun for a "Village" type Museum on 16- acre plot at south end of Kelley Park.

1970 - Work begun on site for outdoor museum (old San Jose 1850-1920) in October. Dennis Peterson apointed curator.

1971 - Statehouse Museum closed- plans begun to build museum in south warehouse. New Museum opened to public June 18, 1971.

The Statehouse Museum opened in 1950 and was located at the Santa Clara Fairgrounds. And that was in the beggining. Now let's turn the next page and dive into the past where we will find a beautiful peaceful park filled with squirrels, birds and an ocassional turkey. We might even see the trolley running and I know we will see many beautifully restored buildings through the behalf of donations, staff and honored volunteers.

This is the DeLuz house, Mr. Disbig. It was at 502 S. 11th Street in downtown San Jose many years ago. Kristena Nelson Deluz wanted the house brought here after she died. Did you know she was a professor at San Jose State University?

No. I didn't know that, Buddy. Did you know it is now the home of the Hellenic Heritage Institute? The home was built about 1905 and was moved here in 1987.

Wow. Inside, Mr. Disbig, are beautiful paintings and artifacts representing Greek culture. Sometimes they have seminars, cooking and dancing classes and have parties here at HSJ.

That's fantastic, Buddy. Isn't that the renovated Pasetta House next door. I here they have 30 or more paintings from San Jose's best known-artists.

They do, Mr. Disbig. The Pasetta house used to be at St. James and Terraine Streets. It was built in 1905. A Yugoslavian couple owned a fruit-drying business and raised nine children in the home. The home was moved to History Park in 1985.

The sign out front reads, The Leonard and David McKay Gallery, Buddy. Leonard Mckay collected paintings and sold some to benefactor Rob Bettencourt. I think the Pasetta House at History Park is the perfect place to show such a fine collection of artistry.

I agree with you, Mr. Disbig. Let's cross the street and check out the Doctor's house.

I think I need a doctor, Buddy. For some reason I've lost all my color. Matter of fact, my clothes are even black and white. I don't feel so well. I think I might faint.

10

Let me start this tour, Buddy.

I thought you said you were sick, Mr. Disbig.

I was until I saw the doctor.

What did the doctor say was wrong with you?

Nothing is wrong with me. He said the creator
of this book was to cheap to pay for color pages
when he had the book published.

Well, he does have a family to support.
Did you learn anything about the Doctor's
House?

Yes I did, Buddy. The house was built in the 1870's
at Main and Benton Streets in Santa Clara. It was
rented to physicians and a dentist practiced in the
back room. It was moved to the Museum in 1966.
The medical instruments inside look really scary.

Good job, Mr. Disbig. Now let's go to the
Portuguese Imperio House. I hear they have
a beautiful altar on the first floor and the
second floor has many historical exhibits.

Did you know the Compass Rose in front is made
of granite? It was dedicated on Nov. 3, 2001 by
the Portuguese Heritage Society of California. It's
a replica of the 130-foot span in Lisbon, Portugal.

On June 7, 1997, Mr. Disbig, the Imperio
was dedicated. It was during the first
annual Portuguese festival. I advise
everyone to stop in and learn the
history. Let's cross the street and
continue, Mr. Disbig.

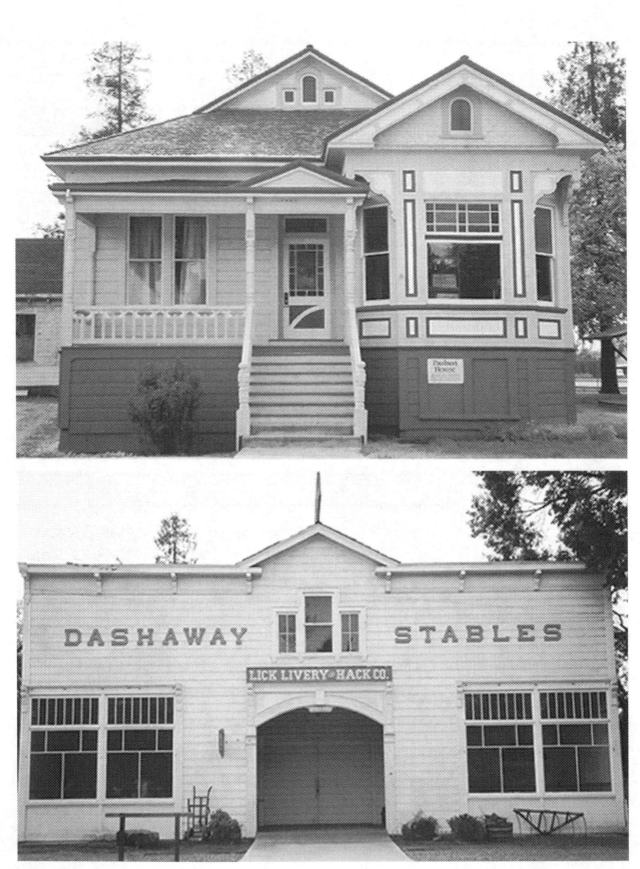

Hey, Buddy. What are you doing?

I'm looking for Mr. Disbig, TedyCat.

I seen him walking over by the hotel. He was looking a little pale.

Yeah. He mentioned something about feeling faint. Is that Mr. Disbig?

I don't think so, Buddy. It looks like a turkey.

Yeah. Right. Well, I'm going to continue looking while I explain the Paulson House. The house was built in the 1890's and located at 343 Prevost St. in downtown San Jose. I think I just saw Mr. Disbig.

That was a Turkey, Buddy. I'll explain the Dashaway Stables if you want to go look for Mr. Disbig, Buddy.

One more line, TedyCat. In 1986, the home was moved to the History Park. The home and family are still being researched as the restoration process continues. Okay, TedyCat.

You want taxi service. You came to the right place in 1888. Located at 130 S. Second Street you could rent different types of vehicles to be pulled by magnificent horses. One of the first later on to provide reservation by phone service. Come tour San Jose with excursions through the beautiful valley. Rent a driver if needed.
Is that Mr. Disbig laying on the ground, Buddy?

I'm going to take a walk over and see if that's him. It looks like it might be a big hotdog they serve at O'Brien's Candy store.

Hello, TedyCat. How are you?

I'm fine, Miss Nay Nay. Where's Buddy?

He's looking for Mr. Disbig. He sent
me over to help you. Besides, I wanted
to tour the Santa Anna School today.

Well, you are a school teacher
for Kidstown School in our book,
"The Adventures of Buddy the Clown
and Mr. Disbig." But first, we need to walk
along this path and visit the Greenwalt House.

That's right, and being a school teacher I know a little
about the Greenwalt House. The house came
to the History Park in 1991. It was built in 1877
in a Italianate farmhouse style, just North of
Highway 85, and west of Almaden Expressway.

Very good, Miss NayNay. I guess I'll let you
tell these fine visitors about the Santa
Anna Schoolhouse while I go look for
Buddy and Mr. Disbig.

Thank you, TedyCat. I'll see you in a little bit.
Santa Anna School, it's beautiful. The wonderful
teachings that went on in this 127 year old,
one-room school after children walked for miles
in the 1890's to get here had to be precious.
Drinking water had to be brought in from neighbors
with pails and the bathrooms, built from redwood,
were then located in back of the school. Since there
was a lack of schools at the time, more were built and
San Jose had one of the first public schools.

Hola, Senorita NayNay. Good to see you. TedyCat
sent me over to help you.

BigDaddy, good to see you again. You
can help me tell the people about the
Zanker House.

Si, Miss NayNay. It would be an honor. The house
was built in the 1860's. William Zanker, from Germany,
lived with his wife and 8 children in the home. In 1986,
the house was moved to the History Park where it was
restored. Out back is a 1906 redwood bathroom which
was located on the original property at Zanker Road
in Alviso.

Eight children. Wow. Now that's why we
need schools. Thank you, BigDaddy.

You are very welcome, Senorita NayNay.
And I must say, all of these homes are very
special and I am proud to thank the people
who have helped History Park maintain the
preservation of this beautiful property.

I agree. This here is another of my favorite
houses, BigDaddy. It is decorated inside
with the 50's theme and furnished like my
parents used to live. Michele Chiechi
bought the home in 1913 and lived in it
for 60 years. It was originally located at
820 Northrup Avenue when it was finally
donated in 1973 to the Museum.

Hola, Senor Meegle, from the planet Mog. It is good to see you, amigo. What brings you to planet Earth?

Meegle visiting Pacific Ocean and all my fish friends tell Meegle, Buddy giving a tour of History Park and Meegle want to help.

Very good, amigo. Gracias. If you like, you can tell these wonderful folks the story of the Umbarger House.

Meegle like to tell story, thank you. In 1851 David Umbarger purchased 136.5 acres off Montery Road. He built this home in the 1870's. The land and home was left to his sister in 1891. The home arrived at the Museum in 1970.

Bravo, Senor Meegle. Would you like to tell another story?

Meegle would. Tell story Meegle know good. Meegle come from planet Mog...

No, Senor Meegle. Not your life story. The story of the Markham home.

Sorry, BigDaddy. Home Meegle think about. Poetry, children activities, library, readings, that's what the San Jose Center for Poetry and Literature use this home for among other delightful programs. Edwin Markham Land Association, in the 1920's, purchased the home. In 1987, it was moved to the History Park.

I think we should get off the trolley tracks before it comes, amigo.

Meegle, say hello to Rascoe. Rascoe good
to see, Meegle like to know how are the
many members of your family?

Meegle. My family is well. All twelve of them.
Buddy sent me over to help you explain the
Hill House.

Very good Hill House is. Explain, Rascoe, my friend,
the legend of the Hill House.

Renowed photographer and artist, Andrew P. Hill,
lived in this home at 1350 Sherman street in 1898.
Some of his paintings are diplayed at the History
Park. The Victorian Preservation Association
sponsored the home and are currently restoring
the structure. The home was moved to the
History park in February 1997.

Tell a story Meegle want. Rascoe tell story good.

You can tell the next story, Meegle.

Meegle come from far far away...

No, Meegle. Perhaps later. Tell the story of
the Post Office.

No mail Meegle get. Meegle like mail.

The Post Office story, Meegle.

Meegle love this story. Back in 1862, when stagecoaches
traveled on the cattle trail between Santa Clara and
San Francisco on Monterey road, this establishment
served as both a bar and post office until 1882. It was
the oldest working post office before it came to HSJ in 1972.

You know, they wanted young riders
to ride horses from St. Louis to
Sacramento to deliver the mail. Rabbits
can run as fast as a horse at short distances.

Grapy. Good to see you. You're looking healthy.

I'm feeling healthy, Rascoe. Nothing like eating the proper foods to keep me trim and fit. Miss NayNay sent me over to help.

Great. I'll tell these wonderful folks about the Gordon House and you can tell them about Stevens Ranch Fruit Barn.

Okay. I love fruit. Wow. Did you see the size of that squirrel? I need to watch out for them. They eat all the good nuts that are healthy for me.

There's plenty of trees here at the History Park for everyone to enjoy. Did you know the author refers to this house as the Rotary Club home because the restoration was funded by the San Jose Rotary Club. They now use it as their headquarters?

No. I didn't. Wow. Look at that big squirrel.

The home was purchased by the Gordon family in 1887. Originally, the home sat at 5303 McKee Road. In 1986, the house was moved to the History Park.

Smell that fruit. Back in 1867, Orvis Stevens purchased the land where this fruit barn sat and by 1892, had grapes, pears, apples and peaches constituting one of the first orchards of Coyote Valley. He dried his fruit in this barn. The barn now houses displays of the past and the progress of Silicon Valley.
There's a squirrel on top of the barn, Rascoe.

We all need to eat. Let him be, Grapy.

Have you ever heard of a killer squirrel?

Hey, Slammer. What brings you to the History Park?

Buddy, sent me. I've come to save the day. I'm here to rescue those whom need to be rescued. I will fly high above and be on the lookout for those who need my help. I have come too...

Okay, okay. Just tell these fine folks about the Empire Firehouse.

I want to save someone.

You will. The Firehouse, Slammer.

In the 1800's Firehouse's were run by volunteers. After a city ordinance in 1854, professionals were required. In 1869, the Empire Firehouse was constructed due to an overwhelming demand of equipment storage space. The Empire Firehouse, located at 375 Second Street, housed the first fire engine of San Jose. A fire, in July of 1892, destroyed the building.

I liked that story. Good job. My turn now. The Electric Tower, as it was named, was the foresight of J.J. Owen. Not only did he want to light downtown San Jose, but he wanted to show others that San Jose was on the edge of modernization. The 237 foot, 24,000 candlepower tower, was ignited December 13, 1881, at the intersection of Santa Clara and Market Streets. A raging windstorm in February, 1915, brought the structure to its knees. This is a replica, standing 115 feet at the History Park.

Wow. I should've told that story. Oh well, too late. I still want to save something. Hey, Grapy. Look at that big squirrel.

Hi, Buddy. Did you find Mr. Disbig?

I was told he went in the hotel. I checked O'Brien's Candy store and the gift shop but could not find Mr. Disbig.

He's probably exploring the park. He'll be back. You want me to talk about the Bank of Italy?

Yeah. Go ahead, Slammer. Did you know the man sitting in the bank was the founder of the San Francisco Bank of Italy?

Amadeo Peter Giannini, in 1904, Buddy. In 1909, the first out of town branch opened. The bank was on the corner of Lightston and Santa Clara in downtown San Jose. Later on, he was to found the largest private bank, The Bank of America National Trust and Savings Association.

Quite a story, Slammer. Before I get to the Pacific Hotel, let's go inside to O'Brien's Candy Store where, in 1878, the first ice cream and soda's were served West of Detroit.

Yeah, I heard about that. In 1868, an Irish immigrant with $500.00 in his pocket, began selling baskets of candy outside the Pacific Hotel. His name was Maurice O'Brien and in 1874, moved to 30 S. First Street in downtown San Jose.

That's correct, Slammer. In 1880, the original Pacific Hotel was at 74-80 South Market Street. This hotel had reading rooms, billiard halls, bath and bar. And I'm sure this is really what the visitors want to hear. $1.00 to $1.50, room and board.

Hey, Mr. Disbig. Where have you been?

I wasn't feeling so well. I went to the Pacific Hotel.

I didn't see you there. Slammer and I just had an
ice cream at O'Brien's Candy Store.

I was up in the conference room sleeping.

Well, you want to talk about the print shop?

No. No. No more talk about black and white. I think
I'll cross the street to the Ng Shing Gung Temple
and take in all its beauty and magnificent exhibits.

Okay, Mr. Disbig. I'll meet you there after I
talk about the print shop. This structure was
built in 1884. Originally located at North San
Pedro and St. John Streets in downtown San
Jose, the false front of this building was
characteristic of old buildings in San Jose.
In 1972, the building was moved to HSJ.

That was quick, Buddy. I guess I'll talk about
"Ng Shing Gung," when translated means;
"Temple of Five Gods." The original building
was demolished in 1949, but the altar, the five
divinities; God of Wealth, Goddess of Mercy,
Queen of Heaven, the Canton City God and
God of War and Justice were preserved. They
are part of the beautiful exhibits preserved by
<u>The Chinese Historical and Cultural Project.</u>

Come on, Mr. Disbig. Let's get you some gas
and then go shoe a horse.

I really don't feel like
shoeing a horse. What
ever that means, Buddy

That's okay, Mr. Disbig. I'll explain the story of
this Associated Gas Station which sat on
the corner of Julian and Market Streets
in downtown San Jose in 1927.
Owned by different private parties
throughout the years, it was finally
scheduled to be torn down.
With the help of volunteers,
the building was saved, and in 1978,
moved to the History Park.

What kind of ice cream did
you have, Buddy?

Strawberry.

I like Rainbow Sherbet.

Do you want an ice cream, Mr. Disbig?

Yeah.

Let me tell the story of the Blacksmith
and then we'll get a ice cream before we
ride the trolley.

The trolley. Forget the ice cream,
Buddy. I want to ride the trolley.
Can I ride the trolley?
Can I? Can I?

Sure, Mr. Disbig. Give me a moment. The Blacksmith
shop was used to repair wagons, shoe horses, make
tools and other instruments from iron and steel
forged over hot coals. Sometimes they have exhibitions
in this shed during festivals at the History Park.

Can I ride the trolley now?

Yes.

Oh, goody.

Hello, Miss NayNay and TedyCat. I guess everyone wants to ride the trolley. Let me tell these wonderful folks about the history of the Trolley Barn and trolley number 143, also known as the Birney.

Hurry up, Buddy. I want to ride the trolley.

Mr. Disbig, let Buddy tell the story.

You be nice to Mr. Disbig, TedyCat. He just wants to ride the trolley. It's okay, Mr. Disbig.

Thank you, Miss NayNay. I'll buy you an ice cream.

Okay, everyone. Anyway. This Trolley Barn was built in 1984. It was built in the tradition of California Barns from the early 1900's. Inside are projects which have been restored with the help of volunteers and the California Trolley and Railroad Corporation (www.ctrc.org). Two of the trolley cars are used here at the park. They plan, hopefully, to extend the trolley tracks to link Kelley Park. This trolley car, #143, ran in Fresno. The St. Louis Car Co. built this in 1922 and was designed to have a single operator. The name Birney, came from the designer, Mr. Charles Birney.

Can we ride now? I want to get on before Mr. Disbig.

One more page, TedyCat. Do I get a soda with my ice cream, Mr. Disbig?

De Luz · Pasetta · Doctor's Office · Portuguese Imperio

Paulson · Dashaway Stables · Greenwalt · Santa Anna School

Zanker · Chicchi · Umbarger · Markham

Andrew P. Hill · Post Office · Gordon · Fruit Barn

Firehouse · Electric Light Tower · Bank of Italy · Pacific Hotel

Ng Shing Gung Temple · Print Shop · Gas Station · Blacksmith

Trolley Barn · Visit www.historysanjose.org · Birney #143

Hey, Grapy. Leave those squirrels alone.

Thanks, Slammer. Hello, everyone. I'm sure you remember all my friends from today. If you would like to see more of them visit your bookstore and ask for ISBN number 1-4010-9050-8 or just ask for "The Adventures of Buddy the clown and Mr. Disbig." You can also visit www.prtproductions.com and save time and money.

Enough about us. We like to think of the History Park as one of the most informative, beautiful, peaceful and serene parks we have had the pleasure to visit. Voted family favorite in 2005 by Bay Area Parent. The History Park provides an ambience of joy and relaxation along with many special events provided to the public.

Here you are openly greeted to a family atmosphere of fun while you learn about days that were before many of us were born. Not only does the History Park offer times from the past, it allows new ones for the future with you in mind.

The pleasure you receive from the staff and from very well-trained and energetic volunteers is overwhelming. Their goal is to please the public and they show that desire by helping everyone to understand these buildings history. If not for these great people along with you, parks like these may not flourish. We invite all of you to come visit the park everyday when the park is open. Either come by yourself or with your family. Visit the events the park has to offer or book your own family event. We have given you brief descriptions of the buildings at the park to find out more come visit HSJ in person or at www.historysanjose.org.Thank you for your time. Now it's time to introduce another of our favorite parks at Kelly Park; the Japanese Friendship Gardens.

Can we ride the trolley now, Buddy?

I still want my ice cream, Mr. Disbig.

Japanese Friendship Gardens at Kelly Park

Six and a half acres of Kelley Park was dedicated as a home for the Japanese Friendship Gardens in 1960. Okayama's world famous Korakuen Garden was used as the design to create the warm atmosphere while placing bridges, rocks, trees and flowers to establish a serene setting. Visitors marvel at the spectacular and breath taking appearance of the park which came together from visitor's like you and other contributions from numerous organizations.

On the 8th anniversary of the Sister City affiliation, in 1965, the Japanese Friendship Garden was dedicated. Keeping with the dream, which started in 1957, when President Eisenhower wished to establish a relationship between other countries and the United States.

The Pacific Neighbors, an organization formed to sponsor as a link between the two-cities, made the original proposed concept to create the Japanese Friendship Gardens.

Inside the park you will see beautiful attractions stemming from a waterfall to trees, bridges, lanterns, a Pagoda, Teahouse, Turtle Island and plenty of Koi fish. Read everything you find because inside this beautiful park, everything not only has a story, but a special meaning as well. Come visit the park and enjoy the traquil leisure the park offers. For more information go to www.ci.san-jose.ca.us/cae/parks

A Haiku poem

I've changed my dwelling
To bathe in Summer coolness
So tranquil, so calm.
—— Paul Iwashita

Happy Hollow Park and Zoo at Kelley Park

In 1961, Happy Hollow opened the doors to become one of San Jose's favorite children's parks and zoo. Surrounded by the community and nestled under beautiful shade trees, this family park offers the public an incredible journey from fabulous picnic areas to marionette puppet shows and maybe the most popular of amusement rides, Danny the Dragon Train. Built by the Arrow Development Co. in 1960 and credited with rides such as Dumbo in Disneyland, this machine shop started with a group of World War II veterans.

Rare and endangered species survive at this accredited institution along with a petting zoo which offers a variety of goats, a Dwarf Zebu, Llamas and other fun creatures for the children to interact with while learning the history behind these very special animals.

Happy Hollow's 12.5 acre park offers a variety of activities stemming from birthday parties to educational programs including summer camp for children. This moderatly priced park and zoo has playgrounds for the entire family to enjoy and offers many special events like Earth Day Celebration and Annual Food Drive.

We are proud to have given you information concerning these favorite family gathering places here at Kelley Park and invite you to come visit these fine facilities which will be able to provide more information of the guidelines set forth to enjoy all the ammenities they have to offer. Not only does Kelley Park have three tremendous establishments inside the park, additionally it offers the Leininger Center, which can provide you with information on reserving other attractive San Jose Regional Parks. Now let's visit two other fantastic museums and then some of those other family parks. Please, get out of the water, Meegle.

The Tech Museum of Innovation is located at 201 South Market Street in San Jose. The three-level facility houses' 132,000-square feet of fun and technology for the entire family, young and old alike, to not only play with some of the most remarkable gadgets but to learn from them as well.

The Tech Museum of Innovation started in 1978, as an inspiration to bring science and technology together for human awareness. Junior League of Palo Alto had a vision to create such a project and later, teamed with the San Jose League to initiate its goals. In 1990, a 20,000- square foot test center opened at the old Convention Center and proven successful has been given a warm reception by visitors alike and a standing ovation from the citizens of Silicon Valley.

Over 2,800,000 visitors have come to see the phenomenal building home to unprecedented exhibits. Workshops and labs allow the visitor to explore leisurely during their adventure while others get involved with the learning potential. "The mind is a limitless void, capable of drawing in and out."

A projected 650,000 each year are expected to visit the creative and gallant structure with a Domed Imax® Theater, a cafe, bookstore, gift shop, educational center and one-of-a-kind exhibits. This infrastructure fills the hearts with progress and capabilities set forth by human nature and the desire to not only learn but to continue to learn and invent for not only today or tomorrow, but for the next generations to come.

Exciting opportunities happen at the Tech Museum of Innovation including awards that were inspired by individuals who developed particular goals. In 2001, the awards were brought forth to accompany the achievement of not only individuals, but also new an old companies wanting to better the world. Awards for environment. Awards for education. Awards for economics, health, communication, agriculture, medicine, jobs, poverty, equality. These are only a small percentage given out each year; more awards can be documented for individual commitments.

The Tech Museum of Innovation has opened a door to progress and with the help of individuals like you can continue its dreams of becoming a learning institution for everyone. Become a member and dwell in the satisfaction that with every little contribution, the world is becoming a better place to live.

BUDDY

*Pictures from Hubble - Credit: Nasa

The Tech Museum of Innovation

The Tech Museum of Innovation

Most of us believe learning should be fun, others think if it's that easy, it's not right. The Tech Museum of Innovation grants you the ability to have fun while you learn. Everything from robotics to exploration of sciences is offered to enhance self-knowledge and awareness.

Visit the Earthquake Platform Shake and shimmy to an 8.4

One of the best ways to learn is to interact; the Tech Museum of Innovation does just that, not only for adults but also for children. One of the most precious sounds you could hear is the laughter of children. Now you can listen to the children laugh as they make their way through the Play Path, an exhibition of discovery and enrichment for the young.

Create your own reality world.

Imagination playground invites the children to learn while they have fun with Glow Stones, a new version of wood blocks responding to signals from other stones. Toy Boxes; learn technology from within the box. Sneak and Spies, clubhouses, one high one low, watch the kids as they listen and spy around the exhibits. Bug Puppets, Shadow Garden and Maraca Motion, these fun adventurous interactives allow first hand knowledge of creativity.

Imagination Playground

The future is bright for all of us and with learning centers like this one. It is a future of excitement for every city, for every person, for the endowment of life that can be carried out to inspire, aspire and create a separate vision for each and everyone of us.
For information call: 408-294-Tech or visit www.thetech.org.

*Map provided at The Tech Museum of Innovation

42

Children's Discovery Museum

Hello, my name's Jack. My brother Buddy wanted me to introduce a very important Museum to everyone. A museum I recently visited called The Children's Discovery Museum. The museum is fantastic.

I was surprised and inspired on how well the museum was set up for the children. And, I saw how every child there was having a delightful good time. They were laughing, playing, jumping and participating in all the activities the museum had to offer.

On the first floor they have WaterWays, these magnificent water games let the children experiment with colorful plastic balls as they invade the water sources and perform to the different actions from the water. They do supply splash gear for the children.

They also have, Bubbalogna, which allows children and adults to experiment with bubbles. They have Current Connections, Kids Garden, Post Office, Rhythm Huts, Step into the Past, Streets, Take Another Look, The Lee and Diane Bradenburg Theater and Zoomzone™ and this is all on the first floor.

On the second floor they have Pizza Please, CdMedia.studio and a wonderful exhibit named, The Wonder Cabinet, a perfect learning center with a responsible staff that allows infants and preschoolers to learn hands on exploring of basic fundamentals. Overall, I can understand why Children's Discovery Museum has won many awards.

I was able to take some pictures of my tour and I would like to share them with you along with a little history that I believe is important, so turn the page and enjoy what I enjoyed. By the way, The Children's Discovery Museum has a large facility which can be used to accommodate almost any party. To find out more call (408) 298-5437 or visit their website at www.cdm.org. Better yet, take a little drive with the family to 180 Woz Way in San Jose, Ca. 95110

JACK

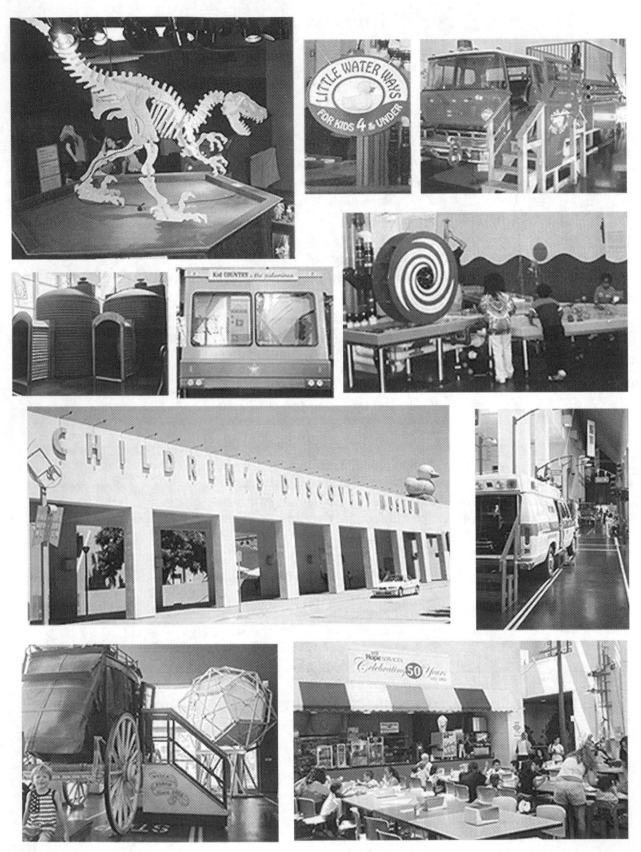

A place where the child must feel that the whole plant is for him, that the best is offered to him because of faith in his power to use it, that he has access to all departments, and that he is always a welcome visitor, never an intruder.
Anna Billings Gallup

* Establishment of board of Directors, September, 1982.
* Establishment of a permanent site with approval (December 1984) by the San Jose Redevelopment Agency of funding allocation to aquire property for the Museum within the Guadalupe River Park.

* Implementation of a comprehensive "Museum on the Road" program, encompassing "Stage Door Stories" (1984) and a traveling exhibit on disabilities, "One Way or Another" (1985) serving more than 40,000 children to date.

* Commencement of exhibit fabrication by Museum staff January, 1988.
* Completion of Capital Campaign, July, 1989 with more than $9.75 million raised.

* Occupancy of the 42,000 square foot facility, January, 1990, designed by internationally renowned architect Ricardo Legorreta of Legorreta Arquitectos, who was also commissioned to design the Quadalupe River Park.

* Celebration of Children's Discovery Museum's public opening, June 2 and 3, 1990.

National Awards:
* Most Promising Pratices Award 2000- Awarded by Met Life Foundation and the Association of Children's Museums recognizing our Summer of Service program.

* National Award for Museum and Library Service- Awarded by the Institute for Museum and Library Services, the highest honor a museum or library can receive for service to its community.

Recognition:
* Child Magazine (2002), "Top Ten Children's Museums"

CHILDREN'S DISCOVERY MUSEUM

Alum Rock Park

Located off Alum Rock Ave. in San Jose, this diverse park offers a family friendly atmosphere with plenty of childrens activities including a museum identifying certain wildlife, plants and floral. Comprised of 700-acres, which include biking trails, walking trails and picnic areas, slides and swings meet the need for children with a nice area for hikers, roller blades and bicyclists.There is a fee attached for cars but you can walk in or bike in free of charge. For more information call: 408-277-5561

Anderson Lake

Located at 19245 Malaquerra Ave. in Morgan Hill, sits 3,109 acres, Santa Clara's largest reservoir, with multiple trails. Power and non-power boats are welcome on the seven-mile long lake and even jet-skis skim by on the placid waters. This beautiful scenic park offers, fishing, picnic areas and barbecue facilities for the entire family to enjoy right on the shoreline. Equestrians use the park along with bicyclists and everyone can enjoy a nice swim on a hot day. For information call: 408-779-3634

Almaden Quicksilver Mines

A landmark of California history, the 4,147 acres offers beautiful wildflowers and 34.2 miles of hiking trails and also a history of over 135 years of mining. Located in the town of New Almaden in South San Jose, the quicksilver (mercury) mines had made fish in the area unsafe to eat. Mining structures throughout the park have been sealed and gates locked. However, comprised of equestrian trails, walking trails, bike trails, a museum and picnic tables, you are still invited to walk your dog. For more information call: 408-268-3883

Calero County Park

Located at 23201 McKean Road in San Jose, the 3,476 acre park offers a breath-taking look at the California Oak woodland. Immersed with beautiful plants and natural wildlife, the recreational activities include sailing, fishing, boating, water and jet-skiing. 18.6 miles are available to hike. Picnic and barbecues span the water's edge. Horse rentals are available at the Calero Ranch Stables. For more information call: 408-268-3883

Chesbro Reservoir County Park

Located at 17655 Oak Glen Road near Morgan Hill, the 216 acre park and man-made reservoir is a haven for fisherman. Black Bass, Catfish, Crappie, Trout and Large Mouth Bass swim in the cool waters where only non-powered boats are allowed. Beautiful calm waters set the theme for sailboats and kayaking. The park has established no designated trails. For more information call: 408-779-9232

*Map provided at www.parkhere.org

Ed R. Levin County Park

Situated at 3100 Calaveras Rd. in Milpitas, golfing, picnicking and fishing are recreational events at this 1,539 acre park. Gorgeous lawn areas stretch through the park making it family friendly while nature-lovers hike and bike through beautiful Oak woodlands. Watch the hang-gliders and paragliders while you fish or sail one of your model sailboats from an inflatable raft. Relaxation is what the park offers with its 19 miles of trails.
For information call: 408-262-6980

Hellyer County Park

Located at 985 Hellyer Ave. in San Jose, this beautiful 205 acre park offers an Olympic-size bicycle racetrack Coyote Creek runs through the park that allows the visitor to explore a scenic route along paved trails. Fishing, hiking and play areas are just a few of the amenities along with grasslands to throw a frisbee or have a barbecue.
For information call: 408-225-0225

Joseph D. Grant

Situated at 18405 Mt. Hamilton Rd. in San Jose sits the largest regional park in Santa Clara County. Beautiful oak trees abound surrounding some of the finest landscaped recreational areas on this 9,553 acre park. Watch the cattle craze, ride a horse, have a picnic or take in a leisurely hike choosing from 52 trails. Several small ponds and a large lake are what the fisherman dream. Reserve one of forty family campsites.
For information call: 408-274-6121

Lake Cunningham Regional Park

Two entrances open into this park, one on White Rd. and the other off Tully Rd. in San Jose. This beautiful 202 acre scenic park was opened in 1982 for family fun and leisure. Rent a paddle boat, a canoe or even a sailboat and explore the 50 acre fresh water lake. Harboring a fitness course, bike trail and walking trail along with picnic areas, this park entertains everyone from young to old. Throw a line in and see if there's bluegill, bass or catfish on the other end. Visit Raging Waters next door where waterslides are the attraction. For information call: 408-277-5351

Lexington Reservoir County Park

Located at 17770 Alma Bridge Rd. in Los Gatos just off Hwy. 17, a 475 acre man-made lake sits awaiting the next fisherman. Available to non-gas powerboats only, you can still launch a rowboat, sailboards or electric powered boats. The 941 acre park provides walking trails that may ultimately connect to several other parks.
For more information call: 408-356-2729

Mt. Madonna County Park

Located at 7850 Pole Line Rd. in Watsonville and surrounded by a beautiful majestic redwood forest, this 3,688 acre park overlooks Monterey Bay. Nestled with grassy meadows and scenic trails, descendants of the White fallow deer, which were donated in 1932 by William Randolph Hearst, wander in an enclosed area for the public to view. Reserve a campsite and have a family barbecue or visit the archery range. Listen to live music at the amphitheater or learn about Indians, nature and cultural history at the visitor's center. Drive in with your RV and relax the nights away.
For more information call: 408-842-2341

Santa Teresa County Park

Nestled above Santa Teresa Golf Course in San Jose, this 1,627 acre park hosts a beautiful spectrum for ecology lovers. Picnic tables and barbecue areas provide relaxation for your group while others may want to ride a horse. Visit the archery range or climb on board a golf cart while visiting the 18- hole course. For more information call: 408-225-2650

Uvas Canyon County Park

Situated at 8515 Croy Rd. in Morgan Hill and housing, twenty-five campsites, the 1,133 acres offers miles of hiking trails while some visit natures waterfalls. Smell the aroma of the spectacular flora while enjoying a nice family picnic. Visit Uvas or Chesbro reservoirs during your stay and explore on a non-powered boat. For information call: 408-779-9232

Vasona Lake County Park and the Los Gatos Creek Parkway

Located at 333 Blossom Hill Rd. in San Jose, a wonderful very family-oriented, 150 acre park looms, inviting visitors to explore all its highlights and beauty. Come paddle a boat, row one, fish, hike, jog or ride a bike along the trails with your dog. This fantastic park has a lot for everyone. Take the children to the playgrounds and ride a carousel, a merry-go-round or ride the Billy Jones Wildcat Railroad. Come have a picnic and throw a ball, kick a ball or settle down and relax with a fishing pole while you observe the parks waterfowl. For more information call: 408-356-2729

*Map provided at www.parkhere.org

"Red Rose" By Paul Trainer 12/21/98 (HillTop Records)

She is standing there with a ribbon in her hair and
in her right hand a red rose.
She looks to see what it all means as she looks at the ground below.
Her dreams were filled with loving him knowing they would never end.
You can see a tear fall from her eye as the memories dance, through her mind.
To touch your hand.
To hold you tight.
To kiss your soft lips once again.
My memories of loving you keep dancing through my mind.
I wonder why they took you away
Just to bring you back this way
The world is good I know in my heart but why did loving have to start
I hear your voice in the middle of the night and hope to wake by your side
To touch your hand.
To hold you tight.
To kiss your soft lips once again.
She is standing there with a ribbon in her hair and in her right hand a red rose.
She looks to see what it all means as she leans over the gray stone
Her dreams were filled with loving him knowing they would never end.
Her hearts at ease and her minds at peace as she drops, her red rose
To touch your hand.
To hold you tight.
To kiss your soft lips once again.
My memories of loving you keep dancing through my mind.

"Fish in the Ocean" Paul Trainer 1983

Golden yellow glitter in the trees, a tall thin man standing by the sea
watching for the sunrise alone in the dark with not much time
Holding everything that is true he dreamed of living with someone like you
but he found out late, now has his doubts, for where he goes no one will know
Fish in the ocean, the moon in the sky, watching for the sunrise
The deep blue ocean is his escape and as the tides roll in they break against the rocks
Time has passed it goes so fast and the seagulls fly so free
Fish in the ocean, the moon in the sky
watching for the sunrise

"Little child on the front line" Paul Trainer 1983

Oh little child on the front line
get off the beach while you still can
the sounds of gunfire coming from all sides
stop the war there's no more reason to die
Oh little child on the front line
the beach is glowing in the moonlight
the sands are covered with bloodshed
get out of site before you are dead
Oh little child on the front line
your mama's crying for you to be found
There's bodies laying to the left and the right
let us hope you escape this night
Oh little child on the front line
with the bombs bursting in the night sky
the sound of shells exploding on the ground
it's great to know America is still around
Oh little child on the front line
you were found still alive
your mama's waiting for you to come home
Oh little child your no longer alone

"Don't give up" by Paul Trainer 1981

When your feeling
your about to give up
when your road is getting
to rough
don't lose your hold on life
because you can take it on in
strides
When your woman she leaves
when you lose her love
and you can't get it back
you got to stay on the right track
Don't give up
No, don't give up
Don't lose, your hold on life
You can live a life of your own
but you must take control
you got to move with the flow
and you can't let go
When you feel your body tremble
in the middle of the night
and you dream of life and
how you held her tight
Don't give up
No, don't give up
Don't lose, your hold on life.

"Moondog over Miami" Paul Trainer 1984

She came out of the fog diffferent from mankind
it was worse then someone could describe
She had four claws walked on two
a sight that would boggle the mind
Moondog, Moondog, Moondog
Moondog over Miami
Heard of her existence from rumors in the night
said she came in and devoured at sight
Moondog, Moondog
Her skin was red she looked like the dead
eyes of doom when she looked at you
Moondog, Moondog, Moondog
Moondog over Miami
She had control of any man she held
stole his soul and crushed his bones
Showed no feelings had no heart
grown men would scream running through the park
Moondog, Moondog, Moondog
Moondog over Miami
She would fight lions and tame the bears
eyes of doom when she looked at you
Moondog
Moondog over Miami

Qty	Description	Price	*S/H	**Ins.	Total
	Buddy the Clown book Signed	$27.00	$3.00		
	Buddy Poster	$20.00	$3.00		
	Buddy Poster Signed	$30.00	$3.00		
	Buddy Fan Club Signed	$5.00	$2.00		
	Buddy Friends Faces Poster	$20.00	$3.00		
	Buddy Friends Faces Poster Signed	$30.00	$3.00		
	Clown Novel Signed	$25.00	$3.00		
*Sold in Bulk	* Learning the History of Kelley Park in San Jose	Inquire at prtproductions @hotmail.com	$.00		
	Learning the History of Kelley Park in San Jose Signed by Author	$20.00	$3.00		
	Screenplays	$500,000.	Free		
	1 Song -8x10- sheet Song Lyrics -Signed	$5.00 *Each*	$3.00		
Message:	*Write song or songs in message*	Total			

	Send Check or Money order to:		
	PRT Productions		
	3697 Norwood Ave.		
	San Jose, Ca. 95148		

Ship to:

Name:

Street Address:

City:

State:

*S/H- $3.00 per item   **Insurance (optional) $1.50 per item
Money order ship next day Checks wait to clear
Free S/H for Orders over $60.00
Order inquiry prtproductions@hotmail.com
Prices subject to change. CA. TAX Rate.

Copy and print shipping form for order.
Send with check or money order
Order online at www.prtproductions.com

Printed in the United States
By Bookmasters

Allographs™ II

Teacher/Parent
Manual

Linguistic Spelling Program

Diane McGuinness

Allographs I Manual, Copyright 1997 Diane McGuinness.
Allographs I and II complete. Filed with the Register of Copyrights,
U.S. Library of Congress, October, 1997. # 098378453
New Revised Edition

Order this book online at www.trafford.com
or email orders@trafford.com

Most Trafford titles are also available at major online book retailers.

Print information available on the last page.

ISBN: 978-1-4251-5782-1 (sc)

Trafford rev. 10/28/2022

Trafford
PUBLISHING® www.trafford.com
North America & international
toll-free: 844-688-6899 (USA & Canada)
fax: 812 355 4082

ALLOGRAPHS II

Allographs II teaches spelling, reading, vocabulary, and grammar. It is designed for students at the third to fourth grade level (ages 8 to 9), as well as for older students and adults who have difficulty spelling multisyllable words. Allographs II teaches the "morphemic level" of the English spelling code. The morpheme is the smallest unit of sound that changes the meaning of a word. English is a compounding language, building words by adding morphemes.

Spellings for common English words are based on the phoneme (Allographs I). The morpheme level of the spelling code adds an extra level of complexity. This is created by root word transformations that occur during compounding, and by multiple spelling alternatives for suffixes. Spelling problems are created, as well, by homophones (words that sound alike with different spellings –hear/here), words with adjacent vowel sounds (po-et, tri-al), the ubiquitous 'schwa' vowel sound, and the expanding number of syllables in words.

Allographs II trains students to master these complexities in simple logical steps. Children learn how to compound words. What can be compounded can also be taken apart. This is the key to reading fluency and good spelling. All English, French, and Latin prefixes and suffixes are taught, as well as spellings for common Greek words. A Word List Supplement introduces students to multiple spellings for Latin suffixes. This provides all the words containing each suffix organized by spelling probabilities. Students can see at a glance which spellings are likely and which are not. Because the morpheme is a unit of <u>meaning</u>, lessons naturally lead to work on grammar and rapidly build vocabulary.

There are 59 lessons in Allographs II. How fast you proceed will depend on the age and the vocabulary level of the students. For classroom teachers, most students can master these spelling patterns in one year (two lessons per week), others may take longer (one lesson per week). Difficulty increases as the lessons progress, and Latin suffixes are the most difficult of all. For parents and for reading specialists, time will depend upon how many hours per week you can devote to the exercises.

The same "sound-to-print" logic used in Allographs I is maintained in Allographs II. Sounds are enclosed in slashes. Please check the following pronunciation key so you say these vowel sounds (phonemes) correctly during the lessons.

PRONOUNCIATION KEY FOR VOWEL SYMBOLS

<u>Sounds</u>	<u>As In</u>
/a/	cat
/e/	bet
/i/	sit
/o/	hot
/u/	cut
/a-e/	made
/ee/	seem
/i-e/	time
/o-e/	home
/u-e/	cute
/ow/	how
/oi/	oil
/oo/	book
/<u>oo</u>/	soon

Consonant symbols use the main spelling for each consonant, including single letters and common digraphs: /ch/ /ng/ /qu/ /sh/ /th/ (thin) /<u>th</u>/ (this)

Manual: Table of Contents

	Page Number
Who is ready for Allographs II?	5
Children's Word Knowledge	6
Using Allographs II	7
Compounding words:	
with 'fire' and 'sun'. Lesson 1	8
with 'land' and 'house'. Lesson 2	9
with ''light' and 'line'. Lesson 3	9
Mix and match. Lesson 4	9
Homophones. Lesson 5	10
Putting homophones into sentences. Lesson 6	11
Special Plurals. /f/ to 'ves'. Lesson 7	12
Adding suffixes to change verbs:	
Verbs spelled: <u>a-e</u>, <u>i-e</u>, <u>o-e</u>, <u>u-e</u>. Lessons 8-11	13
Verbs sounding /a/ /e/ /i/ /o/ /u/. Lesson 12-16	14
Verbs ending <u>ve</u>. Lesson 17	15
Verbs ending <u>ge</u> and <u>dge</u>. Lesson 18	15
Multi-syllable verbs ending /ul/. Lesson 19	15
Multi-syllable verbs ending /ee/. Lesson 20	16
Multi-syllable verbs ending /ie/. Lesson 21	16
Add <u>y</u> to make an adjective. Lesson 22	17
Turning verbs into persons. Lesson 23	18
Suffix potluck. Lesson 24	19
Answers to Worksheet 24	20
Adjacent vowel sounds: 2 syllables. Lesson 25	21
Adding prefixes:	
de re Lesson 26	22
pre pro Lesson 27	23
be e Lesson 28	23
im in Lesson 29	23
em en Lesson 30	23
Adjacent vowel sounds: 3 syllables. Lesson 31	24

Table of Contents page 2

	Page	Word Lists
Multi-syllable words ending <u>ine</u>. Lesson 32	25	
Multi-syllable words ending <u>ite</u> or <u>ice</u>. Lesson 33	26	
Multi-syllable words ending 'schwa.' Lesson 34	27	
Unscrambling schwas and prefixes. Lessons 35-38	28	
Multi-syllable words ending <u>ate</u>. Lesson 39	29	
Changing verbs to nouns with <u>ment</u>. Lesson 40	30	
Changing adjectives to nouns with <u>ive</u>. Lesson 41	31	
Adding <u>ive</u> when root word changes. Lesson 42	32	
The Latin/French suffix <u>ous</u>. Lesson 43	33	
Schwas in the middle of words. Lesson 44	34	
Word List Lessons:	35	
The suffix 'er'. Lesson 45	36	1
The suffix 'airy'. Lesson 46	37	2
The suffixes 'unt' and 'unce'. Lesson 47	38	3
The Latin suffix 'shun' spelled <u>tion</u>. Lessons 48-52	39	
The Latin suffix 'shun' more spellings. Lesson 53	40	4
The Latin suffixes 'shul' and 'shuh'. Lesson 54	41	5
The Latin suffix 'shus'. Lesson 55	42	6
The Latin suffixes 'shunt' and 'shunce'. Lesson 56	42	7
Suffixes with the sound /zh/. Lesson 57	43	8
Spelling /ch/ in Latin words. Lesson 58	44	9
Spelling /j/ in Latin/French words. Lesson 59	45	10
Lessons for Greek words	46	14-15
Table of common irregular verbs	47	
References	48	

Who is Ready for Allographs II?

Allographs II is designed for children and for poor readers and spellers who are spelling at about the third-grade level (age 8 to 9). It focuses on multi-syllable words, up to and including the Latin and Greek layers of our language.

Allographs II builds on the skills attained in Allographs I or any good phonics program that teaches spelling alternatives for each sound. Students should have mastered the following skills:

1. Knowledge of 40 sounds or "phonemes" in the English language and the spelling alternatives for each sound in common words.

2. The ability to segment, blend and spell common English words at the CCVCC level of complexity, up to and including two-syllable words.

3. The ability to read text at the two-syllable word level and to identify all the spelling alternatives for a particular sound in that text.

4. Knowledge of basic orthographic tendencies in common words:
   a. Consonant spellings that differ in the initial or final position in a word: <u>v</u>an, car<u>ve</u>; <u>th</u>em, ba<u>the</u>.
   b. Vowel spellings that vary with the position of the vowel in single and multi-syllable words: str<u>ee</u>t, carr<u>y</u>
   c. Final consonant spellings 'controlled' by the preceding vowel sound: scree<u>ch</u>, ca<u>tch</u>; gou<u>ge</u>, fu<u>dge</u>.
   d. Double letters stand for one sound: dress, battle.

5. Knowledge of the common patterns for English spellings. This means knowing which spellings are more likely than others:
   '*seem*' but not 'seme' or 'siem.'

6. Able to spell from dictation common one and two syllable words.

The same guidelines apply that were important in Allographs I.
   Sounds are in slashes **/b/**, and spellings are underlined <u>**b**</u>.
   Avoid letter names unless they are scripted into the lesson.
   Avoid spelling rules.
   Use simple, precise language.
   Keep the correct logic throughout: **Sounds are real. Letters are arbitrary (unreal) symbols for sounds in words.**

Children's Word Knowledge

Children's vocabulary increases rapidly from the age of six to ten years. When children were shown videos containing lots of new words, they were able to remember these words after hearing them only once. When they were retested later on, they could remember the words and their meaning almost perfectly (Rice and Woodsmall, 1988).

Anglin (1993) studied the types of new words that children learned. The spurt in vocabulary growth was not due to adding more root words. Root words only increased from around 5,000 to 7,500 words, and new idioms added a mere 500 more words. Most of the vocabulary growth was due to an increasing understanding of how words can be compounded by prefixes and suffixes to change their meaning. When compounded words were counted, vocabulary skyrocketed to 35,000 words.

Anglin called this new type of language development "morphological problem solving," the ability to analyze word parts to get at meaning. The "morpheme" is the smallest unit of sound that can change the meaning of a word. The letter s at the end of a word is a "morpheme." It changes the meaning to "more than one." In the word "happier," er is a "morpheme" meaning "more happy than before." 'Happiest' means "the most happy one." A language that uses prefixes and suffixes to change meaning is called a "compounding language." English is a compounding language. So is Latin and Greek.

Over half the words in the English language today are based on Latin words. The Latin root contains the core meaning; the prefix marks a change in meaning ('not' 'more' 'under' 'over') and the suffix marks a part of speech, like noun, verb, or adjective. Most Latin roots are no longer in use or even understood. Instead, Latin words are compounded. For example, the Latin root 'struct' means "to build." 'Construct' means to "build with," 'instruct' means "to build in." 'Instruction' is the noun form; 'instructing' the present participle of the verb. And the list goes on: structure, superstructure, restructure, destructive, and so forth.

Allographs II is based on the natural development of children's language and the compounding nature of our language. This makes it possible to understand how to read and spell words by learning how words are put together. Knowing which parts are units of meaning is critical, because many elements of the English spelling code are based on these morphemic units. As children discover how to separate words into their component parts and put the parts back together, this improves reading fluency as well as spelling. It adds an important new dimension to the logic of the alphabet code.

Using Allographs II

The lessons in this manual will guide you to the best use of the workbook exercises. However, there is no limit to your creativity in making these exercises come alive. This would include searching text for examples of what has been taught, using each lesson as a springboard for creative writing, for learning about grammar, and for increasing vocabulary.

Lessons are partially scripted. Each lesson contains the goals to be taught, and the workbook exercises are tailored to meet those goals. Every student must have his or her own workbook. **Follow up every lesson with some spelling dictation using the words in the exercises.**

Use fiction or non-fiction texts at the appropriate level to provide more practice. For example, when you finish simple word compounding, ask students to search text for compound words, copy them out, and present them to you or the class. Try to instill an atmosphere of mutual help and enthusiasm for learning about how words work, and what words mean. *Encourage everyone to become a "wordsmith"* and dazzle Mom and Dad with their expertise.

As the lessons increase in complexity, use your judgement for how much support to provide. In some cases, you may need to do the entire exercise together, especially with some of the difficult Latin words. Classroom teachers can let children help each other to find the answers to the workbook exercises. But insist that every child completes each exercise, with or without help. Practice is essential, because spelling is as much about <u>really</u> looking and visual memory, as about learning spelled patterns determined by parts of speech and meaning. Understanding these concepts will build by practice.

For parents or clinicians working individually with a student, adapt the lessons for one-on-one instruction. You can use a small whiteboard, or a pad of white paper. Extra help may be needed, especially if the student has been having trouble learning to spell. If you find you're giving so much help that you're actually doing the exercises for the student, use Allographs I before proceeding further. Understanding how common English words are spelled, and awareness of the spelling alternatives at this basic level, is essential to a smooth transition to spelling the words in Allographs II.

Adults who need additional help with their spelling can do these lessons on their own. Follow the manual and do the worksheets. Get a family member to give you some spelling dictation at the end of each lesson.

Compound Words. Lesson 1

Goals: Learn about compounding two real words .

The next few lessons are about compounding simple English words into new words. Note that these compound words are not hyphenated.

"In our language we can put words together to make a new word. These words are called "compound words." [Write 'compound' on the board.] Let me show you what I mean. [Write the word 'dog' on the board.] The word 'dog' means a kind of animal. [Write the word 'house' on the board.] The word 'house' means a place where people live. But if you put the two words together like this: [put 'doghouse' on the board] it means a place where a dog lives.

Sometimes compounding completely changes the meaning to something totally new. [Put the word 'hot' on the board.] If I combine 'hot' and 'house' [put 'hothouse' on the board] then I am talking about a house that is hot. It's where plants live. But if I combine 'hot and 'dog' [put 'hotdog' on the board] I do not mean a dog that is hot. I mean something new, a kind of sandwich.

Open the Workbook to Worksheet 1. All the words in the list can join with the word 'sun' or 'fire' to make a new word. Figure out which one is correct by saying the words out loud. Let's start with the word 'fly'. Say 'sunfly'. Does that make a word? [NO]. What about 'firefly'? Is that a word? [YES] OK. Now you finish the rest of the words."

Activities: 1) Ask students to make sentences using these words. For older students this is not necessary.

Spelling dictation.

Compound Words. Lessons 2 and 3

Goals: Same as Lesson 1.

Introduce these lessons in the same way. It may not be necessary to do an example. Point out that some of the words have the front part missing, and some have the back part missing. It is helpful to say these words out loud to decide which is correct.

Worksheets 2 and 3.

Compound Words. Lesson 4

Goals: To find words that will compound with another word.

This task is more difficult, because the student has to read the first part of the word, and then read through the list to find the best match to make a new compound word.

> **Now that you're all expert in compounding words, we're going
> to do something more difficult. Open the Workbook to Worksheet 4.
> The words on the left side can only compound with one word
> on the right side. Here's how to do this exercise.**
>
> **What is the first word on the left? ['after']. Now let's go down the
> list on the right side together. Is 'aftercake' a word? "Afterroad"?
> 'Afterstack'? 'Afternoon'?**

Hopefully, someone will recognize that 'afternoon' is a word. Ask them to write the word 'noon' next to the word 'after' and then cross 'noon' off the list on the right. They should continue on their own with the rest of the list. This is a good exercise to do in small groups.

Activities:
After Lesson 4, ask students to be on the lookout for compound words in books that they are reading. If they find any, they should write them down and present them to you or to the class at the next spelling lesson.

Spelling dictation.

Homophones. Lesson 5

Goals: To learn what a homophone is. To learn some spellings for common homophones.

There are homophones in every language. This is where two identically sounding words mean totally different things. You can only understand the meaning of the words when they are used in context. Most writing systems mark these words differently, so that the spelling itself provides a further clue to meaning. English is no exception.

This lesson asks students to identify the vowel spellings in pairs of homophones. This will be easy for everyone if they have completed Allographs I. If not, then you will need to offer more help.

> **There are lots of words in English that sound exactly alike but mean completely different things. We call these words 'homophones' [write 'homophone' on the board]. This is a Greek word, and it's a compound word too. 'Homo' means "same" and 'phone' means "sound." Homophones are words that have the 'same sound.'**
>
> **Let me give you an example. Suppose I say that last weekend I went to the woods and saw a bear standing in a bare field. How do I spell the word 'bear' meaning the animal? [Ask for suggestions. Put the correct spelling on the board.] What about the word 'bare' which means 'uncovered.' [Ask for suggestions, then put this on the board.] Homophones are hard to spell. You have to memorize which spelling goes in which word.**
>
> **Open your Workbook to Worksheet 5. Here are pairs of homophones. Find the vowel in each pair of words, and underline the vowel spellings. Let's do the first pair together.   What is the spelling for the /e/ (bed) sound in 'bear' the animal? [Ans. ea. Put it on the board.] And the /e/ sound in 'bare', meaning uncovered? [Ans. a-e. Put it on the board.] OK, now underline the letters that stand for the sound /e/ in these words.   Now finish the rest on your own.**

[Note: Students who have been through Allographs I will know this vowel as 'air,' a "vowel + r" pattern with 5 spellings: 'bear' 'bare' 'chair' 'arrow' 'cherry.' It's OK to underline the whole vowel+r (ear are). There are nine vowels that combine with the sound /r/ to produce one vowel. In Allographs I, four from this group are specifically taught because of multiple spelling alternatives.]

Spelling dictation.

Homophones. Lesson 6

Goals: To be able to spell homophones correctly in context.

If these homophone spellings are too unfamiliar, turn this into a dictionary exercise. Use a good children's dictionary. Have students work in small groups or pairs to speed things up. Older students can do this worksheet without a dictionary.

Last time we looked carefully at how some homophones were spelled. Today we're going to use these homophones in sentences. Open your Workbook to Worksheet 6. Each sentence has two missing words. You have to decide which of the two homophone spellings is correct and fill in the blanks.

If you don't know these spellings very well you will have to use a dictionary. You might want to work with a partner, or the other children at your table.

Let's do the first one together. We know that the sentence reads: 'John heard a herd of goats in the field.' This means that there was a group of goats, or a 'herd', which were making some noise that John could hear. Which spelling of 'heard' do you think is correct for John's ability to hear the goats? Which spelling is correct for the word that tells us there was a group or 'herd' of goats?

If the students have no trouble with this example, then let them proceed on their own through the worksheet. If they are struggling, then tell them to use a dictionary, and help them work out what to do.

Activity.
Follow this up immediately when they finish the Worksheet. Review each sentence in turn. Go over the meaning of every homophone and make sure that they understand the meaning of the words <u>and</u> the sentences.

Spelling dictation.

Special Plurals. Lesson 7

Goals: Learning how to add plurals to words ending in the sound /f/. Sometimes the root word has to change and sometimes it doesn't.

Adding plurals to words isn't always straightforward. As noted earlier, sometimes you add 's' and sometimes you add 'es'. In order to know what to do, you have to listen to the word carefully to hear how it sounds before your write it down. In this lesson, the students learn to add plurals to words ending in the sound /f/. Sometimes the letter 'f' is changed to 'v' and sometimes it isn't. Also, there are four possible spellings for the sound /f/. Students need to say the plural form out loud to decide which is correct, and even then, the task isn't easy.

We learned before that when we change words into plurals, we mean more than one. Most of the time it's easy to turn a word into the plural. Just add the letters 's' or 'e' 's' to the word. Once in a while adding plurals can be difficult, because you need to change the ending of the word.

Open the Workbook to Worksheet 7. All these words end in the sound /f/. This sound can be spelled four different ways. To change these words to the plural you have to be a good listener. Sometimes you have to make a change to the word first and sometimes you don't. Look at the first example.

I could say that a little elf came to help me clean the house. But if more than one showed up, I would have to say that some 'elves' came to help. If I said 'some elfs' or 'some 'elfses' it wouldn't sound right. So you need to do some careful listening to do this exercise.

It's a good idea to make up a sentence to fit the words into, like: I saw one elf, then I saw five elves. I saw one 'calf', then I saw five ------?-----. See if you can finish this exercise on your own. If you aren't sure, then check in the dictionary.

Answers: <u>dwarfs</u> <u>chiefs</u> do not take the 'ves' ending.

Spelling dictation.

Adding Suffixes. Lessons 8-11

Goals: Learning to add suffixes to verb roots which represent 'ongoing action' (present participle) and past tense. Learning how to add suffixes to root words with the vowel spellings: <u>a-e</u> <u>i-e</u> <u>o-e</u> <u>u-e</u>.

Your students may or may not know something about verbs and verb suffixes. Modify these lessons to suit their knowledge. You may need to present a more extended lesson than is provided here.

The vowel digraphs listed above can be split apart by one consonant --but not two-- and still work together. (There are exceptions, but not many.) When these words take suffixes, the final <u>e</u> is dropped, and the vowel in the suffix substitutes for the missing <u>e</u>. This keeps the main vowel sound constant. This is one of the few times that English spelling patterns ever come close to a 'rule.' Use shortened version of this lesson for the remaining Worksheets in this group.

You all know what a 'verb' is. It is a word in a sentence that describes actions, thoughts, feelings. When we say that John runs home, 'runs' is the verb. When we say that Suzy thinks too much, 'thinks' is the verb. A verb is whatever somebody does.

Verbs have different endings for when we're describing something happening now, in the past, or in the future. If I say 'I <u>bake</u> bread.' This means it's something I can do. But if I say, 'I am <u>baking</u> bread,' this means that I am doing it right now. It's an ongoing action. I will keep on doing it until I'm finished. When I am finished baking bread, I can say: 'I <u>baked</u> some bread today.' This means the bread was baked in the past. The baking is over.

These endings are called 'suffixes.' [Put 'suffix' on the board.] Adding suffixes is also called "compounding" too, just like we learned before. The difference is a suffix doesn't make any sense by itself. It only works with a 'root word' and not alone. We're going to work with the suffixes that change verbs to 'ongoing action' or to 'past tense.'

On Worksheet 8, these verbs are spelled with the digraph <u>a-e</u> [put on the board]. You have to drop the 'e' to add a suffix.

Activities: Ask students to choose a few of these verbs and use all three forms (present, present participle, past tense) to create written sentences.
Complete Worksheets 9-11 in this set.

Spelling Dictation

Adding Suffixes. Lessons 12-16

Goals: To learn how to keep the same vowel sound when adding suffixes to verbs spelled with one vowel letter.

The 'rule' about the first vowel in a suffix substituting for the missing letter <u>e</u>, is still working when you add suffixes to verbs that have <u>a single vowel letter</u> in them. As an example: bat, bating, bater. To solve this problem, you must double the final consonant. This cancels the control over the main vowel by the vowel in the suffix. Thus, you write bat, batting, batter.

This "doubling rule" never applies if the main vowel is a digraph ('beaming'), or with an adjacent vowel combination ('rioting'), or in any multi-syllable words that end in 'er' 'en' 'et' or 'el ('suffering,' 'listening,' 'marketing,' 'paneling.')—**but** does apply in similar type words where the accent is on the second syllable ('occu<u>rr</u>ing')! Children cannot remember rules, especially those with complex or negative logic. Avoid this problem entirely, as shown below. Your language is very important.

> **We have been adding suffixes to verbs that end in the letter 'e'. Today we're going to learn how to add suffixes to some other verbs. The most important thing about these verbs is that they have only one vowel letter in them.**

> **Open the Workbook to Worksheet 12. Here is a list of the verbs I'm talking about. Look at the first word 'bat'. If we just added the suffix 'ing' to this word, we would have this: [put 'bating' on the board]. This says 'bating.' It isn't the word we want. We're trying to spell 'batting'. Can you tell me what you have to do to get 'batting' instead of 'bating'?**

The clues are contained in the instructions and the examples. Let students study this for a while, and see if they can figure out what to do. If not, give them the answer. Finish with a clear definition.

> **So, in verbs like these, little short words with only one vowel letter, if you add a suffix, you must double the final consonant to keep the same vowel sound. You can finish this exercise now.**

Continue on with the remaining lessons in this set. **Use Worksheets 13-16**.

Spelling Dictation.

Adding Suffixes. Lessons 17-19

Goals: To learn about the remaining verbs that need spelling transformations.

These lessons focus on various spelling issues that arise when adding suffixes to root words. Use your judgment in presenting these new exercises. Here are the issues for each of them:

Lesson 17. The final <u>e</u> in <u>ve</u> is there because of spelling convention: All words ending in the sound /v/ are always spelled <u>ve</u>. You add suffixes in the same way as in Lessons 8-11 by dropping the final <u>e</u>.

Lesson 18. This is the same issue. Final /j/ is never spelled <u>j</u>, but always <u>ge</u> or <u>dge</u>. Just drop the letter <u>e</u> and add the suffix.

Lesson 19. Now there is a mixture. If the word ends in <u>e</u>, it is dropped. If the word ends in a consonant, add <u>ing</u>. Consonants do not have to double in these words, though either spelling is technically correct (canceling, cancelling). The final syllable in these words is the same sound (a schwa+/l/). It can be spelled several ways. [Allographs I has lessons on this family of words. They are difficult to spell.]

Worksheets 17-19

Spelling dictation.

Adding Suffixes. Lessons 20 and 21

Goals: To learn how to add suffixes to verbs ending in the letter y. To learn how to add suffixes to verbs ending in the sound /ie/.

When a multi-syllable word ends in the sound /ee/, it is usually spelled with the letter y. This is nearly always true for verbs. (Exceptions are words where /ee/ is spelled ey: volley, jockey, journey, monkey.)   The verbs keep the final /ee/ sound when adding a suffix. BUT the y remains when adding ing, and changes to i in adding ed, as in tally, tallying, tallied.

> **Open your Workbook to Worksheet 20. Here are some verbs that end in the sound /ee/. It's spelled with the letter 'y'. Let's look at the example on the top line. The letter 'y' stays when you add the suffix 'ing' but it changes to the letter 'i' when you add the suffix 'ed'. Let's read the first three words together.**

> **'bully' 'bullying' 'bullied' Notice that we don't say 'bully-ed' do we? The same is true for all the words in this list.**

> **As you do this exercise, be sure to say each word quietly to yourself. Let's read all the words together first.**

Define words they don't understand.

Activities: Have students put some of these words (all three forms) into sentences. **Worksheet 20.**

Spelling dictation.

Lesson 21

Ask students to look at **Worksheet 21**, and notice the two ways to spell the sound /ie/ in these words. Next, they should notice that no matter how they are spelled, they look the same after the suffixes are added. In the list of words at the bottom, the ie spelling changes to y before adding 'ing'.

NOTE: There is a list of common irregular verbs at the end of this manual if students haven't learned these spelling patterns. You can do this as a board exercise. Write the present tense on the board and ask for the past tense in a verbal exercise like: "Today I go. Yesterday, I ___"

Adding Suffixes. Lesson 22

Goals: To learn how to change words into adjectives by adding the sound /ee/ spelled y.

If your students don't know what an adjective is, you will have to spend more time on this than provided by this lesson.

Adding the suffix y to words is a common way to change nouns and verbs into adjectives. But this isn't straightforward. If the word ends in the letter e, then this must be dropped. Adding y sets the 'vowel control principle' into operation. The letter y acts on the preceding vowel, backwards across one consonant but not two. Cancel this 'vowel control' by doubling the final consonant.

Today we're going to learn a way to turn words into adjectives. [Put 'adjective' on the board.] An adjective is a word that describes something. These are words like 'nice' 'mean' 'green' 'strong' 'kind' and so forth. We can make adjectives by adding the suffix 'y' to some nouns and verbs. The suffix stands for the sound /ee/.

You can't make all nouns and verbs into adjectives. Let's put some on the board. [Put on the board: tub, table dirt, rob, grass, house, shine, fish.] I'm going to add the letter 'y'. Let's see if this makes a real word:

Write on the board: tubby, tably, dirty, robby, grassy, housy, shiny, fishy. Ask the children which are words and which are not.

So this works sometimes and not others. I want you to notice what I had to do to add the letter 'y' to some of these words. For 'tubby' I had to double the last consonant, otherwise it would have sounded 'tooby'. For 'shiny' I had to drop the final e.

Open the Workbook to Worksheet 22. Every word in this list can be turned into an adjective by adding the letter 'y'. Remember to drop all final 'e's, and remember that you may need to double the final consonant. If you aren't sure, then look the word up in the dictionary.

Activities: Have students write stories using some of these adjectives.

Spelling dictation.

Adding Suffixes. Lesson 23

Goals: To learn how to use the suffix <u>er</u> for adjectives and for turning verbs into 'persons.'

The suffix /er/ is the most common suffix in English. It operates to increase the emphasis of an adjective: green, greener. It changes verbs (the action) into the person doing the action (the actor).

Today we're going to learn about a new suffix. We can use it to change adjectives to mean "even more so" like in the words 'green' 'greener'. Suppose I said: "My brother is mean." Then you might say: "But my brother is _____.

You tell me some adjectives and I will write them on the board.

Use your judgement for how much time to spend on this activity. When several adjectives are on the board, see how many can take the suffix 'er'. It is so common, children may not need to spend much time on this.

Now let's talk about another way to use the same suffix. We can change verbs into 'persons' with the suffix 'er'. Open your Workbook to Worksheet 23. Here is a list of verbs. Everyone of them can be turned into a person by adding the suffix 'er'. For the word 'bake', someone who bakes is called a 'baker'.

Be careful. You need to remember to drop a final 'e', and sometimes you must double the final consonant to make the vowel sound stay the same.

Activity: Have students write a story about some of the 'persons' in this list. You can make it a competition by having the one who uses the most persons, wins.

Spelling dictation.

Adding Suffixes. Lesson 24

Goals: Practice with common English suffixes.

There are many common English suffixes. Most are spelled exactly as they sound. Those that begin with a vowel require the same changes we have already learned about with <u>ing</u> and <u>ed</u>. Research has shown that children use common suffixes accurately, even though they don't know what a 'suffix' is.

> **Today we're going to learn about lots of suffixes.**
> **There are some we learned before, plus many new ones.**
> **They are all common suffixes that you use every day when**
> **you talk, but you probably haven't thought about it before.**
>
> **Open the Workbook to Worksheet 24. Across the top is**
> **a row of suffixes. Some of these suffixes can be added**
> **to the words in the list, and some cannot. You can tell**
> **which ones will work, by adding the suffix to the word**
> **and saying the word out loud. If it doesn't make any**
> **sense, then it's wrong.**
>
> **Let's try the first one together. Is 'brightable' a word?**
> **[NO] OK. So this won't work, will it? How about 'brightance',**
> **'brighted', 'brighten'——?**

Hopefully, someone will know that 'brighten' is a word. If not you will have to tell them. Ask them to put the word 'brighten' in a sentence. If they can't, then suggest something like: "We bought some flowers to brighten the room."

This is an excellent Worksheet exercise to do with a partner or in groups. Depending upon the level of interest and difficulty, you may want to do the second page on another day. (**Answers** on the next page.)

Activities: 1) Students should put all the words in a set into written sentences when they finish. Allow plenty of time for this activity.
2) If you are working with an older student or an adult, you might want to review parts of speech. Do this after the entire exercise has been completed, and then go through each word individually: brighten (verb), brighter (adjective), brightest (adjective/superlative), brightly (adverb), brightness (noun).

Spelling dictation

Answers to Worksheet 24.

bright	brighten brighter brightest brightly brightness
pity	pitiable pitied pitiful pitying pitiless
fresh	freshen fresher freshest freshly freshness
care	cared careful caring careless
turn	turned turning
fine	fined finer finest fining finely
face	faced facing faceless
pose	posed poser posing
enjoy	enjoyable enjoyed enjoying enjoyment
excite	excitable excited exciting excitement
hope	hoped hopeful hoping hopeless hopelessness
happy	happier happiest happily happiness
fool	fooled fooling foolish foolishness
sad	sadly sadder sadness saddest
dirty	dirtied dirtier dirtiest dirtying
move	moveable moved mover moving movement
form	formed former forming formless
like	likeable liked liken liking likely likeness
state	stated statehood stating stateless stately
cheer	cheering cheered cheerful cheerless
wonder	wondering wonderful wondered wonderment
base	based baser basest basing baseless basement
kind	kinder kindest kindly kindness
firm	firmed firmer firmest firming firmly firmament firmness
place	placed placing placement
clean	cleaned cleaner cleanest cleaning cleanly

Adjacent Vowel Sounds. Lesson 25

Goals: To learn how to segment words with adjacent vowel sounds, and to identify syllables.

Words are hard to read and spell when two vowel sounds are side-by-side. This is especially a problem when the two vowel letters commonly represent a vowel digraph and usually work together to stand for one sound. This exercise alerts students to this group of words, so they will become more familiar with them and will be more able to read and spell them correctly.

> **We're going to do something different today. We're going to learn about words with two different vowel sounds side-by-side. These words are hard to read and hard to spell too.**
>
> **If you open your Workbook to Worksheet 25, you'll see a list of these words. Every word in this list has two syllables in it. Each syllable needs a vowel, doesn't it? The vowels in these words are side-by-side. This can be confusing to read, because many of them look like one vowel and not two.**
>
> **Look at the first word. We know that these letters [Put <u>o-e</u> on the board] stand for the sound /oe/ most of the time. But in this word, they stand for two separate vowel sounds. If I read it the usual way, it would sound 'pote' which is wrong. Do you know what it says?**

Give them the answer if they don't know.

> **Notice that there is a line separating the two syllables. This line comes in between the two vowel letters. Your job in this exercise is to find the two vowel letters and draw a line between them, and then read the word out loud. After this, copy each word, and separate the syllables, like the example. When you've finished, we'll read the words together.**

At the conclusion of this exercise, you should go through the word list. Ask individual students to read each word. Pronounce it correctly if they did not. Define words if necessary.

Activities: Use the dictionary to look up the meaning of any words students do not know. Have them put some new words in written sentences.

Spelling dictation.

Adding prefixes. Lesson 26

Goals: To learn some common prefixes. To discover that many roots that take prefixes aren't a word by themselves. Beware: these lessons are a higher level of difficulty than anything so far.

Prefixes that are common in English are common in Latin and French derived words as well. Most of the root words in this exercise are Latin and French. They make no sense in English, but combine with prefixes (and suffixes) to make common English words.

Today we're going to start something new. We will be learning about prefixes. [Put 'prefix' on the board.] A prefix is like a 'suffix' except that it comes at the beginning of a word instead of at the end. A prefix is part of "compounding" too.

Open the Workbook to Worksheet 26. This is an exercise for adding the prefixes 'de' or 're'. The prefix 'de' means to go against, or to undo something, or 'entirely'. The prefix 're' means to do something again. If you 'repeat' a grade, it means you have to do it again.

Notice that a lot of the base words, or 'root words' don't make any sense. These words are from the old French and Latin languages. We borrowed thousands of these words into English, but only the compounded words and not the roots.

Let's do the first word together. The root is 'bate'. This word is from the French 'battre' which means 'to beat' or 'bring down.' We don't have to know this to do this exercise, but it is interesting. Will 'bate' make a word if you put ''de' or 're' in front of it? Is 'debate' a word [YES]. Is 'rebate' a word? [YES]. This means you can use either one to put in the blank.

After the students finish, provide the correct answers. If students are interested in word derivation, explain that 'debate' literally means to 'go against to try to beat' and 'rebate' literally means to 'bring down again' (meaning the price).

Activities: Have students look up the meaning of words they don't know in the dictionary. They can select some words to put in written sentences.
For older students or adults interested in word origin, let them check on the meaning of the root words in a good dictionary.

Spelling dictation.

Adding Prefixes. Lesson 27-30

Goals: Same as lesson 26.

The prefix lessons continue in the same format for the next four lessons.

When you introduce each lesson, be sure to point out the meaning of the prefixes set out at the top of the worksheet. Always define every word at the end of the lesson, or ask students to define the words, and/or look up the words in the dictionary.

Students can use words they choose to create written sentences.

Worksheets 27-30.

Spelling dictation.

Adjacent Vowel Sounds. Lesson 31

Goals: To be able to segment words of three-syllables that contain adjacent vowel sounds.

This lesson is similar to lesson 25, except it's considerably harder. To read these words, the student has to locate the adjacent vowels, find the strong syllable in the word, mark it, and finally to pronounce the word correctly. Identifying strong and weak syllables in words becomes essential when students move to text that contains words of three syllables or longer. They must hear syllable boundaries in order to decode the word, and where the syllable accents go, in order to get at meaning. *Be aware that there is no magic formula for where syllable boundaries go. Students must mark them according to what they hear.*

> **If you open the Workbook to Worksheet 31, you'll see a list of words that have two vowel sounds side-by-side. We've seen words like this before. This time, the words are three syllables long. So this exercise is much harder.**
>
> **First, you have to read the word and find the two vowel <u>sounds</u> that are side-by-side. Draw a slash mark between them. Next, draw a slash between any other syllables in the word. Use your ears to decide where this goes. Then draw a line under the strongest syllable in the word.**
>
> **The first word is done for you. The word is 'deity'—which means 'God.' The syllables are de-i-ty. Listen for the strong syllable.**

Say 'de-i-ty' again and emphasize the strong syllable. Ask someone to try the next word (don't say the word). Put 'violin' on the board. Have a student decide where the slash marks go, write it on the board with dashes, and underline the main syllable.

> **In the instructions it says that the letter 'i' can stand for three different vowel sounds. You'll have to try each of them.**
> **What does 'i' stand for in 'de-i-ty' [Ans. /i/]. In 'vi-o-lin' [Ans. /ie/]**

Some students may find this exercise very difficult. Pair them with a good student, work with them individually, or work with the entire class.

When everyone is finished, review each word. Say each word correctly. Define unfamiliar words, or extend this into a dictionary exercise.

Spelling dictation.

Multi-syllable Words Ending <u>ine</u>. Lesson 32

Goals: To be able to recognize the various ways that the ending <u>ine</u> can be pronounced in multi-syllable words.

This is the first of three 'suffixes' that overlap with root word endings. Because of this, it isn't a good idea to teach this as a suffix. The suffixes are of French and Latin derivation, but **ine** closes many common English root words, like 'fine' and 'dine'. The sounds of the suffix were borrowed as well. The pronunciation for Latin words is **/een/**, for French - **/in/**, while for English, it is **/ine/.**

This is much too complex to teach and wouldn't help spelling anyway. Instead, students learn a group of words ending in the same spelling which has three possible vowel sounds. The task is to sort the words under the correct sound symbol.

There are lots of words that end in this spelling [Put <u>ine</u> on the board.] This ending happens in a lot of words, and doesn't mean anything special. There is a problem reading and spelling these words, because the vowel letters in this ending can stand for three different vowel sounds.

If you open your Workbook to Worksheet 32, you'll see what I mean. Your job is to read each word, mark the syllable boundaries, like it shows you, then underline the strong syllable. You'll have to say the word out loud to yourself to figure out where it comes. When you have finished this, then say the word and listen carefully to the sound of the last syllable.

Does it have the sound /ee/ (seen) in it? If it does, then write the word in the first column. Does it have the sound /ie/ (tie) in it? If it does, then put it in the middle column. Does it have the sound /i/ (pin) in it? If it does, then put it in the last column.

We'll do the first few words together. What is the first word?

Spelling dictation.

Multi-syllable Words Ending <u>ite</u> or <u>ice</u>. Lesson 33

Goals: To be able to recognize how <u>ite</u> and <u>ice</u> are pronounced at the ends of words. To use your judgement in splitting syllables.

These are French and Latin derived words where there is more than one way to pronounce the final vowel sound. There are two sets of words here. As before, these endings overlap with common English root words like 'bite' 'kite' spice, dice, containing the vowel sound /ie/.

Many words in this set have ambiguous syllable boundaries. No one solution is correct.   To learn to read and spell these words, s*tudents should mark boundaries where they <u>hear</u> them*. For example, 'definite' can be split: **de-fin-ite, de-fi-nite, def-in-ite, def-i-nite.**   In other words, this is an <u>auditory</u> exercise, and not an exercise to identify word parts, or in how to comply with a style manual. This logic also applies to double consonants which represent only one sound. They should not be split.

> **Open the Workbook to Worksheet 33. There are two groups of words here. The first group ends in these letters: [put <u>ite</u> on the board.] and the other group in these letters: [put <u>ice</u> on the board.] You can pronounce the vowel sound in these endings, three different ways.**
>
> **Look at the first example. You should mark the syllable boundaries first, then underline the strong syllable. The first word is de-fin-ite. The syllables are split one way here, but there is no right or wrong way to do this. Mark the syllable boundaries where you hear them. [Put the four examples above on the board and discuss this.] Also, remember that double consonants stand for only one sound.**
>
> **Notice that the strong syllable is the first syllable in 'definite.' What is the sound of the vowel in the last syllable? Is it 'defineet', 'definight' or 'definit'?**

Wait for an answer. Ask for questions and clear up any confusion before starting this exercise. Put students who may have difficulty with a good reader and speller, or work together with them, or work with the whole class.

When the students are finished, go over each word together. Either define the words, or ask them to look up the words they don't know in the dictionary.

Spelling dictation.

Multi-syllable Words Ending in a Schwa. Lesson 34

Goals. To be able to spell multi-syllable words that end in a 'schwa.'
To practice segmenting words into syllables.

A 'schwa' is an unaccented /uh/ sound in the weakest syllable in a multi-syllable word. Students taught Allographs I will know what a 'schwa' is. If this is not the case, you will need to spend more time teaching this concept than this lesson provides.

> **How many of you know what a 'schwa' is?** [wait for hands].
> **Well, for those of you who don't know, a schwa is a very weak
> vowel sound that comes on the weakest syllable in a word. It
> always sounds /uh/ no matter how it is spelled. In the word
> 'invitation' the vowel sound in the second syllable 'vuh' is a schwa.
> Listen again: 'invitation'. Do you know how the schwa is spelled?**
> [wait for answers] **In this word it is spelled with the letter 'i'.**
> [Put 'in-vi-ta-tion' on the board, and circle <u>vi</u>] **But a schwa can
> be spelled lots of different ways. The schwa is the hardest sound
> to spell because it's the hardest sound to hear, and is spelled so
> many ways.**
>
> **We're going to do a lot of exercises with the 'schwa' sound,
> starting with Worksheet 34. Let's look at it now. This is
> an easy exercise because the 'schwa' is always in the same
> place and always spelled the same way.**
>
> **There are two and three syllable words in this list. Put slashes
> between each syllable according to <u>what you hear</u>. Then
> underline the strongest syllable. Remember that double
> consonants stand for one sound. There are four words that
> have two vowel sounds side-by-side. Watch out for them.**
>
> **U.S. only. At the bottom of the worksheet, there is game for thinking
> of the names of states. Lots of state names end in a schwa.**

Answers: Alabama, Alaska, Arizona, California, N. and S. Carolina, N. and S. Dakota, Georgia, Florida, Louisiana, Indiana, Iowa, Minnesota, Montana, Nevada, Oklahoma, Pennsylvania, Virginia.

Define any words in the word list that students don't know, or have them look up these words in a dictionary.

Spelling dictation.

Unscrambling Schwas and Prefixes. Lessons 35-38

Goals: To learn that an initial 'schwa' is always spelled <u>a</u>. To decode words where the letter <u>a</u> is a schwa or part of a prefix.

Many words begin with the letter <u>a</u>. This can stand for a 'schwa' or form a prefix with the following consonant. Most of these prefixes are Latin (ab, ac, ad, etc.). This group of words causes spelling problems because sometimes the same two letters are a prefix (**ac-count**) and sometimes they aren't (**a-cross**). There is no way to tell the difference from how the word sounds: *'a-ccount' 'a-cross.'* This means that visual memory is critical for spelling many of these words.

> **We're going to learn about some more schwas in the next few lessons. These are schwas that always come at the beginning of words. Lucky for us they're all spelled with the letter 'a'. This time though, the schwas are mixed up with prefixes where the letter 'a' isn't a schwa. Your job is to figure out which is which, and to try and remember how to spell these words.**
>
> **Let's look at Worksheet 35 in the Workbook. This has the 'a' 'b' and 'a' 'c' words on it. Find the syllable boundaries, mark them with a slash and underline the strong syllable. When you've finished with this, then circle the first letter <u>only</u> if it's a schwa. A schwa is the weakest vowel sound in the word and sounds like /uh/.**
>
> **Remember that double consonants stand for one sound. There's one exception: when a second 'c' stands for the sound /s/. [Put 'ac/cess' on the board.]**

Note: There are other schwas in these words. For older students or adults, you might ask them to circle these as well.

Lessons 36-38 are identical to this one. Use your judgment for how fast to proceed.

Use Worksheets 36-38.

Spelling dictation.

Multi-syllable Words Ending ate. Lesson 39

Goals: To become aware of the two vowel sounds in multi-syllable words ending ate.

Many words end in the letters ate. It is not a suffix that consistently marks a part of speech. The word can be a noun, verb, or adjective. In multi-syllable words that end in the spelling ate, sometimes the vowel is a 'schwa', and sometimes it sounds like 'ate'. Children can only tell the difference between the two if they know the words. You may need to do this as a vocabulary lesson first, and then proceed to the exercise.

> **There are lots of words that end in this spelling. [Put ate on the board.] Sometimes we say this ending sound just like it is spelled 'ate', and sometimes we say it like a schwa-- 'ut'. There's no way you can tell this by looking. You have to know how to pronounce the words. Try both ways and listen to what sounds right.**

> **Turn to Worksheet 39. These words have to be sorted into two groups, depending on the ending sound. Two words have been sorted for you. The first one is 'senate' and the second one is 'vibrate.' Try to do this exercise on your own. If you have trouble pronouncing some words, then look them up in a dictionary, or ask for help.**

Be sure to go over pronunciation and define these words at the end of the exercise. Ask students to notice that the words pronounced 'ate' are verbs. Words ending /ut/ are nouns and adjectives.

Activities: This is a good exercise to look at parts of speech, and write sentences using these words.

Spelling dictation.

Adding Suffixes. Lesson 40

Goals: Using the suffix 'ment' to change words into nouns.

**Today we have an easy exercise. Look at Worksheet 40.
You have to add the suffix 'ment' to all these words. Every
word in the list is a verb, and adding 'ment' to these words
turns them into nouns.**

**The vowel in this suffix is a schwa, so it's actually pronounced
'munt' and it always comes on the weakest syllable in the word.
This is an easy exercise, and you should never have any trouble
spelling words that end in 'munt'.**

**Add 'ment' to each of these verbs, then mark syllable boundaries,
and underline the strong syllable in the word.**

When the students are finished, define words they don't know, or turn this into a dictionary exercise. Ask students to use several of these words in written sentences.

Spelling dictation.

Adding the Suffix _ive_. Lesson 41

Goals: To learn words that are turned into adjectives and nouns by adding the suffix _ive_.

This is an Old French suffix added to Latin root words. It mainly changes verbs and nouns into adjectives, plus a few verbs into nouns. This is a good exercise to sort into nouns and adjectives when it is completed.

> **Turn to Worksheet 41. Here is a new suffix that changes root words into adjectives and sometimes into nouns. We'll decide which is which at the end of the exercise. Your job is to add the suffix to these root words first. Drop the final 'e's off words before you add the suffix.**
>
> **Mark the syllable boundaries, and underline the strong syllable _after_ you add the suffix to each word. The suffix changes the position of the strong syllable in many of these words. We'll talk about this later. If you don't know where the strong syllable is, then leave it blank for now.**

When the students finish, ask individuals to read each word aloud. Check that the syllable accent is correct.   On every word, where the syllable accent changes, stop and point this out. This happens with the following words:

narrate/narrative   percept/perceptive   execute/executive   object/objective subject/subjective   cooperate/cooperative   operate/operative secret/secretive impulse/impulsive progress/progressive

Point out that 'abuse' /z/ can also be pronounced with a final /s/ as well – as in "He was tired of the abuse."

Activity: Mark the words 'N' or 'A' depending on whether the word is a noun or an adjective. You may need to do this with the students. Have them choose words to put into written sentences. Nouns are: _detective, narrative, executive_, and '_collective_' can be either.

Spelling dictation.

Adding the Suffix ive. Lesson 42

Goals: To learn how to add the suffix ive when the root word has to change.

There are two exercises in this lesson. In the first, the change is systematic. In the second, it is very irregular. Decide whether your students are ready for this more difficult exercise, or do it together.

> **We're going to do some more work with the suffix 'iv' today. Open the Workbook to Worksheet 42. There are two exercises here. The first one is fairly easy and the second one is very hard. Let's do the one on the left first. All these words can be changed from verbs to adjectives by adding the suffix ive.**
>
> **If you look at the example you'll see that something has to change in the root word. Can you see what happens?**

After discussion, tell them that in every case, the letters '<u>d</u>' '<u>e</u>' must be dropped, the letter '<u>s</u>' added, and then the suffix. This is a complex change, but it is consistent for all these words. Tell students not to do the bonus words for now.

When they are done, point out that in every case the strong syllable stays in the same place, with or without the suffix. Go through the list and have individual students read the root word and then the transformed word aloud.

> **Now let's look at the next group of words. Every one of them has a different change to add the suffix 'iv.' In the example, the sounds /i/ /t/ have to be added. We can't say "addive". Instead, we say "add-i-tive."**

This exercise is better for older students. Or you might want to do it together with the student or the class. When this exercise is finished, point out that in Worksheets 41 and 42, the full suffix is actually 'tive' or 'sive'.

Answers to bonus words: adhesive   attentive   cohesive   competitive conservative   deceptive   destructive   permissive   retentive   sensitive submissive

Spelling dictation.

The Suffix ous. Lesson 43

Goals: To become familiar with the suffix ous. More practice in marking syllable boundaries and syllable accents.

The Latin/French suffix ous turns root words (usually nouns) into adjectives. These roots are often common English words too. The lesson expands to include four and five syllable words. You may need to work with the students to do this part of the exercise. The trick is to mark off the ous first, and then work with what is left. There are adjacent vowels in these words too, so students need to be made aware of this.

We're going to learn about a suffix that we use all the time. This suffix is pronounced 'us'. It's always on a weak syllable and it's always spelled like this: [put ous on the board.] What do we call a vowel when it's in the weakest syllable and pronounced /uh/. [ANS. a 'schwa.']

This is another schwa that is always spelled the same way. Look at Worksheet 43. Here are lots of words that all end in the suffix 'us'. This suffix turns the root word into an adjective. Two and three syllable words are at the top. The four and five syllable words at the bottom are very hard to read or spell.

Your job is to mark the syllable boundaries, find the strong syllable and underline it. We know that the last syllable is always spelled the same, so mark this syllable first. You'll notice that some words have two vowel sounds side-by- side, like we learned about before. So be careful. If you think you can do the hard words, then go ahead. If not, just wait, and we'll do them together later.

After the exercise, review all the words with the class. Define words they don't understand, or use this as a dictionary exercise.

Activities: This is a good group of words to look for common English root words. They are fairly easy to spot. Tell students to get out a piece of paper, and write down all the common root words they can find in the <u>first set of words only</u>. The second set are compounded with Latin prefixes.

Answers. Set 1 only: marvel envy peril fame blaspheme pore grief number humor riot hazard hide pity glutton slander ponder murder prosper doubt tedium study glory fury ruin danger vigor glamour rapture ardor strength pomp wonder monster nerve disaster

Schwas in the Middle of Words. Lesson 44

Goals: To familiarize students with the many ways that the schwa can be spelled in the middle of words.

Schwas lurking in the middle of words are everyone's spelling downfall. Even the best spellers have to look them up from time to time. One trick is to learn the word with the most common decoding of the vowel letter in the first place, then the spelling is most likely to stick. You'll see what this means below.

Today we're going to tackle the hardest words of all to spell. Even most adults have trouble with these words. There is a trick though, which I'll show you in a minute. Open the Workbook to Worksheet 44. Notice that these aren't very hard words to read. Your job is to mark these words in this order. First, mark syllable boundaries. Then underline the strong syllable. Next, find the weakest syllable in the word and circle the vowel in that syllable. This vowel is a 'schwa.'

You'll notice that the schwa is spelled five different ways. The next thing to do, is to write the words under the heading below based on how the schwa is spelled in the word. Let's do the first word together.

The first word is 'hesitate.' Put it on the board. Ask students where the syllable marks should go and put them in. Find the strong syllable. Find the weakest syllable that has the sound 'uh' in it and draw a circle around the vowel.

The best way to remember how to spell these words, is to pronounce them exactly as they are spelled when you read them in books. For example, if we say the word 'hesitate' quickly and in a sloppy way, then it sounds: 'hezuhtate.' But if we say the word more carefully and clearly, we can pronounce this word like it is spelled: hez-i-tate.

Let's do this for all the words in the list. Who wants to go first?

Students may want to do the exercise with a partner, or in small groups, because it is difficult.

Activities: Put some of these words into written sentences.

Spelling dictation.

Word List Lessons

The Student Worksheet Book contains a 'Spelling Dictionary' for common Latin and French suffixes. This is set out in the "Word Lists" at the back of Worksheet Book. Nearly all lessons from this point are based on these Word Lists. Note that the majority of the lessons are about *suffixes* only, as the spellings of Latin and French *prefixes* are highly consistent with English spelling.

There are many different exercises you can do with the Word Lists. Some ideas are presented in the following lessons. As there are no worksheets for most of these lessons, students should use separate pieces of paper. **Don't let students mark on the Word Lists because they can be used in several different ways.**

Note that one set of Worksheets remains. These are for the various root transformations for writing/spelling the suffix **tion.** They are quite complex, and have been sorted into "families" to help students learn them more easily. Follow the Lessons order, and insure that students start on the Word List lessons *before* they do the last few Worksheets. Do check the Student Workbook sequence and the Manual carefully before you move on.

To learn how to spell words compounded with French and Latin suffixes, students need multiple exposure to many, many words. Overlapping exercises have been provided to ensure consistent exposure and active involvement in writing, spelling, etc. Spelling requires practice (repetition) of all the critical behaviors that make memories stick. This means looking carefully (sorting, underlining, marking), copying words (looking and writing), finding word meaning (dictionary work), writing from memory (creative writing), as well as rote memorization for spelling dictation.

The following pages offer some guidelines for lessons at this more difficult level. Please use your imagination to incorporate this material into other activities.

The page number next to the heading refers to the Word List page. These pages are at the back of the student Workbook, and numbered 1-15.

The Suffix 'er' Lesson 45 Word Lists pg. 1

We met this suffix before when students turned verbs into "persons." It is the most common English suffix there is. It is a common suffix in Latin and French words too. When we borrowed these words, we kept the original spellings. There are three ways to spell the suffix 'er' and no way to decide which to use. This is purely a visual memory problem, and only solved by repetitive use. Here are some suggested activities for students to become familiar with 'er' spelled **ar** and **or**.

Search tasks:

1. Look for "people" words and copy these words onto a separate sheet of paper.

2. Look for animal words and copy these words.

3. Look for object words and copy these words.

4. Make up a story with either the people words, or the animal words.

5. Search text in books, poems, etc. to find words that end in the sound /er/.

Spelling dictation.

The Suffix 'airy'. Lesson 46. Word Lists pg. 2

There are two ways to spell the Latin suffix 'airy'. This suffix doesn't signify much, as these words are both nouns and verbs. There are two goals for teaching these words: First, the spelling **ary** only applies to Latin words which are four or more syllables long. Second: There are only four words in the group spelled **ery.**

Tell the students that when very long words end in the suffix 'airy' they are almost always spelled **ary.**

Suggested activities:

1. Copy words onto a sheet of paper and mark syllable boundaries, and underline the strong syllable. Circle any schwas.

2. Put each word into a sentence.

3. Copy out all the nouns, then all the adjectives.

Spelling dictation.

The Suffixes 'unt' and 'unce'. Lesson 47. Word Lists pg 3

The French suffixes 'unt' and 'unce' usually stand for adjective and noun respectively. Many of these words can be converted from one to the other simply by swapping suffixes. They are consistent in keeping the <u>a</u> or the <u>e</u> in the swap.

Spelling these suffixes is a problem because the vowel is a schwa. You can stress the most accurate pronunciation for the sound /e/ (spelled <u>e</u>), but it is unnatural for people to pronounce the suffix **ant** or **ance** like it's spelled, and /uh/ seems more natural: 'abundunt' 'assistunt'

Students need practice writing these words. Try to think of as many ways as possible that this can be accomplished. Here are some suggestions:

1. Word twins: Find all the words that match in the ant/ance group and copy them out on a sheet of paper. Do the same thing with the ent/ence group.

2. Word solos: Find all the words that <u>don't</u> have a match, that are "solo" words in any of the four groups. [This is hard, and students will need to work together or with you.]

3. Using words from any of the four groups (one group only) create a story using as many of these words as possible.

4. Copy out the words that are unfamiliar and look up the meaning in a dictionary.

Spelling dictation.

The Latin Suffix 'shun' spelled <u>tion</u>. Lessons 48-52

Worksheets 45-49 and Bonus Page.

This common Latin suffix turns root words into nouns. There are over 500 words with the spelling **<u>ation</u>** alone (information, nation, investigation, formation, sensation, etc.), and thousands of words ending **<u>tion</u>** (corruption, inspection). Although **<u>tion</u>** is by far the most common spelling, there are six other ways to spell this suffix, including the French words 'cushion' and 'fashion'.

There are two central issues in teaching this suffix. First, the spelling **<u>tion</u>** is used most of the time. Second, when this suffix is added to a root, quite complex transformations can occur. These transformations are controlled by the ending of the root word. For this reason, we revert to the Worksheet format, which is the best way to teach this. The Worksheets are organized into common patterns or "families" of root word transformations. [Note: There are no tables of words ending **<u>tion</u>**. There are just too many of these words.]

Suggested activities:

1. For this lesson we go back to the **Worksheets section at Lesson 45**. Before students start on these Worksheets, ask them to think of multi-syllable words ending in the sounds 'shun'. Get lots of them on the board. Underline the spellings for the sounds 'shun' in the words so far. Point out that the most common spelling for this Latin suffix, is **<u>tion</u>**.

2. Now ask students to turn back to the Worksheet section of the Workbook to Worksheet 45. Tell them that there is a series of Worksheets for how to add the suffix 'shun' spelled **<u>tion</u>**. Each Worksheet teaches common patterns or "families" of root words which have different ending sounds. The ending sound determines how the suffix is added to the root words. For instance, In Worksheet 45, only **<u>ion</u>** has to be added.

3. Continue with the remaining Worksheets. The instructions and examples show what to do.

Spelling Dictation

The Latin Suffix 'shun.' Six More spellings. Lesson 53

Word Lists pg 4

Suggested Activities:

1. Open the Word Lists section to page 4. Tell the students that <u>all</u> common words ending 'shun' with these spellings are on this page. These can be classified so the students know which spelling to use. Tell them: 1. The second most common spelling is **sion.** 2. The spelling **cian** is only used for an occupation or person. 3. The other spellings are rare. All the words with rare spellings are on this page.

2. Make students familiar with the kinds of words that take the spelling **sion.** First, have them copy out all root words that are a common real word: These words are:

access, admit, aggress, apprehend, ascend, commit, comprehend, compress, compel, concede, concuss, condescend, confess, convulse, decline, depress, digress, discuss, dissent, emit, expand, express, expel, extend, impress, obsess, omit, oppress, permit, possess, pretend, process, profess, progress, propel, recess, regress, remit, repulse, secede, submit, succeed, suppress, suspend, tense, transgress, transmit.

Have students call out what they found. Get <u>all</u> the words above on the board. Students should add any words they missed.

Next, have students put these headings on the first line of a fresh piece of paper: **ess mit end el ede/eed.** Root words with these endings are most likely to take the **sion** spelling. Have students copy each word from the list of root words under the appropriate heading. Next, they should add the suffix **sion**. Circle any words in the root word list that are left over. [Left overs are: concuss, convulse, decline, discuss, dissent, expand, repulse, tense]   Work out together how these root words can be transformed.

2. Make up a story using as many 'persons' or 'occupations' as possible.

3. Copy out the rest of the words with the rare spellings. Look up the meaning in the dictionary.

Spelling dictation.

The Latin Suffixes 'shul' and 'shuh'. Lesson 54.

The Latin suffix 'shul' changes root words into adjectives, and it does so by double compounding, adding 'shul' to roots that have 'ance' or 'ence' suffixes, for the most part. There is no pattern or logic to these spellings. Fortunately, there aren't many words like this, so they are easy to memorize.

Suggested activities:

1. On a separate piece of paper, have students write out the 'shul' words, mark the syllable boundaries, and underline the main syllable.

2. Put words back into their previous root form: 'circumstance'

3. Working alone, or in groups, have students put each word in the 'shul' group into a sentence. They will need to look up many of these words in a dictionary first.

4. Have students write out definitions for the remaining 10 words on this page.

Spelling dictation.

The Latin Suffixes 'shus'. Lesson 55. Word Lists pg.6

Here are all the words that end in the Latin suffix 'shus', a suffix that changes words into adjectives. Many are very difficult words, so students may want to skip those they can't read, or don't know.

Tell the students that all the words that end in this suffix are on this page. Unfortunately, there are five ways to spell this suffix.

Suggested activities.

1. Have students copy out every word they can read, or that looks familiar. Put a list of these words on the board: The list should contain these words: atrocious, delicious, ferocious, gracious, judicious, malicious, officious, precious, precocious, spacious, suspicious, tenacious, vicious, vivacious, voracious, plus any others they want to include. If students don't have all these words on their list, they should copy in the extra words.

    Do the same for the next group: ambitious, cautious, conscientious, fictitious, nutritious, pretentious, repetitious, superstitious.

    Copy <u>all the remaining words</u> with different spellings onto the list as well.

2. Have students mark syllable boundaries in these words. They should know that <u>cious</u>, (and the other suffix spellings) is <u>one</u> syllable. So they should mark this off first.   Without this syllable, the remaining word is only one or two syllables long.

3. Students should look up all the words they don't understand, and put each of these words into a written sentence.

Spelling dictation.

The Latin Suffixes 'shunt' and 'shunce'. Lesson 56

Word Lists pg 7

This table contains all the words spelled with these Latin suffixes. Students should copy them out, mark syllable boundaries, underline the strong syllable and look up the ones they aren't familiar with in the dictionary. They should be able to use every word in a written sentence.

Suffixes With the Sound /zh/. Lesson 57 Word Lists pg.8

This is a sound that hasn't been taught before. Students do not learn this sound in Allographs I. The sound **/zh/,** as you see, has no direct symbol in English, because it isn't part of the old English language. It comes to English from French, and though the suffixes taught in this lesson are Latin, they have retained their French pronunciation for over 900 years!.

Before you can do any exercises with this group of words, you must teach the sound **/zh/**. Explain that you are going to teach some words that have a sound in them that students may not be aware of. This sound is **/zh/**, like in the word 'television.' People know how to say this sound, even though it isn't used in many words. Get everyone to say **/zh/** and listen to the sound it makes. It's important that students practice, because they can't spell the sound **/zh/** if they can't hear it and aren't aware of it.

Have everyone open to the Word Lists at page 8. Here are all the words that have the sound **/zh/** in them in our language. Most of the time this sound appears as part of a Latin suffix, spelled **sion**. Remind them that this spelling also stands for the sounds 'shun' as well. Ask them to notice that 'zhun' is only spelled **tion** in one word. If they want to spell the words on this page correctly, they will have to be able to hear the difference between 'shun' and 'zhun.'

The words at the top of the page are Latin suffixes, the words in the middle are a mix of Latin and Greek words, and the words at the bottom are direct borrowings from modern French. Have individual students read these words aloud.

Suggested activities:

1. Have students copy out the words they know from the top group (Latin suffix). Skip the countries.   Combine student lists at the blackboard to end up with something like: collision, conclusion, confusion, decision, delusion, division, evasion, excursion, explosion, illusion, invasion, occasion, persuasion, precision, revision, seclusion, subdivision, supervision, version, vision, television, artesian, equation.

2. Have students use some of these words in written sentences.

3. Have them copy out all the French words and use each word in a sentence. They should look up the meaning of unfamiliar words in the dictionary.

Spelling dictation.

Spelling the Sound /ch/ in Latin Words. Lesson 58

Word Lists pg. 9

The Latin suffixes we have been learning about originally began with the sound **/t/** or **/sh/**. The French modified some to **/zh/,** and the English changed some to **/ch/.** This is a function of ease of pronunciation in one's native language. In case you don't believe this, try saying the words in the 'chur' and 'choo' group with a clearly articulated **/t/** instead of **/ch/:** 'ad-ven-t-ure.

The students should have no trouble at all hearing the **/ch/** at the beginning of the suffixes or in the middle of a word ('choo'). But you can see that reading and spelling will suffer if they are not made aware that there is a sound **/ch/** in them, and that there are several ways to spell the sound **/ch/** in these words. Try to clarify these issues as you teach this group of word.

The first sixteen words can be taught quickly. Students can copy them out, define them, and so forth. Point out that these are the only words spelled like this.

The 'cher' group is more problematic because this suffix overlaps with common English words spelled <u>cher</u> or <u>tcher</u>, as in 'archer' and 'pitcher.' This problem is increased by the fact that most words ending 'cher' are the same syllable length. The student has to learn these spellings entirely by practice and familiarity, in other words, by visual memory alone.

Suggested activities:

1. Words with the suffix 'cher'. Most of these are familiar words. Have students copy about 20 they choose. They should mark off the suffix from the rest of the word, mark other syllable boundaries, and underline the strong syllable.

2. Words with sound 'choo'. The spelling <u>tu</u> is one full syllable. Many of these words have adjacent vowels. Have students copy every word that contains adjacent vowel sounds, then mark syllable boundaries, and underline the strong syllable.

Spelling dictation.

Spelling the Sound /j/ in Latin/French Words. Lesson 59

Word Lists pg. 10

The sound **/j/** is always spelled **ge** or **gi** in these words. The **ous** ending should be familiar. If not, remind students they have seen it before.

There isn't much complexity here and few words to remember. Carry out the usual exercises with this group of words. Ask students to notice some overlap in the words: religion, religious, contagion, contagious.

Latin Roots and Prefixes. Word Lists. pp. 11-13

There are hours of games you can play by combining Latin roots with prefixes and suffixes, and searching for Latin roots in the word lists and working out what the word really means. This will depend entirely on the vocabulary level and enthusiasm of your students. These kinds of tasks appeal mainly to students who are interested in language, word meaning, and word play.

Word-building.

Put a Latin root at the top of a blank page (or on the board). Students can try, first from memory, to expand roots with suffixes and prefixes. Then they can turn to the prefix page, and then look back through the suffix exercises.

Example: aud/audio (hear, listen) can combine with prefixes and suffixes to make:

audition, audit, auditor, auditory, auditing, audience, audible, inaudible, auditorium

Example: 'rupt' (break, burst):

abrupt, bankrupt, disrupt, rupture, ruptured, corrupt, corruption, corrupting, corrupted, corruptness, corruptible, non-corruptible, erupt, erupted, eruption, erupting, interrupt, interruption, interrupted, interrupting, interruptible

Word Search

Using the tables of Latin words, search for root words in the word lists. Use a dictionary if the root isn't listed in the root table. Using suffix and prefixes, try to figure out the literal meaning of the word.

Greek Words and Spellings Word Lists pp 14-15

Although thousands of Greek words have entered our language, they have not dominated in the way that Latin words have done. Most of these Greek words were borrowed into science and medicine rather than into the common language. This is fortunate, because people during the Renaissance decided to spell them differently, and they would have caused even more spelling problems than they do at present.

There are two tables of Greek words for study. One lists all the academic disciplines or "ologies". This is a good list for the whole class to use with a dictionary, and find out what all these words mean. The other table contains common words with "Greek" spellings. Students should be made aware that Greek is a compounding language, mainly with whole words rather than with prefixes and suffixes, i.e. similar to 'hotdog.'

Students who have completed Allographs I will have met most of these spellings already, all in fact, except the last four. The best type of exercises for these words, is to copy them out by group, and underline the spelling for the target sound. Syllable boundaries and main accents can be marked. Students should look up any words they don't understand, then write sentences using those words.

Interested students can use the dictionary to identify the meaning of the root words in these words. Only a good dictionary provides this information.

Table of Common Irregular Verbs

Only the present and past tense forms are given.

am	was	bleed	bled
is	was	breed	bred
are	were	feed	fed
have	had	flee	fled
get	got	lead	led
give	gave	speed	sped
go	went		
run	ran	creep	crept
eat	ate	keep	kept
sit	sat	leap	leapt
fall	fell	sleep	slept
meet	met	sweep	swept
make	made	weep	wept
see	saw		
hear	heard	dive	dove
feel	felt	drive	drove
deal	dealt	ride	rode
kneel	knelt	strive	strove
stand	stood	weave	wove
shake	shook		
take	took	bite	bit
wake	woke	do	did
break	broke	hide	hid
strike	struck	slide	slid
fly	flew		
sell	sold	bend	bent
tell	told	lend	lent
hold	held	send	sent
drink	drank	spend	spent
sink	sank		
stink	stank	bring	brought
speak	spoke	buy	bought
write	wrote	catch	caught
steal	stole	fight	fought
tear	tore	teach	taught
wear	wore	think	thought
choose	chose		
lost	lost	swim	swam
shoot	shot	win	won

References

Anglin, J. M. (1993). Vocabulary development: A morphological analysis. Monographs of the Society for Research in Child Development, *58*, 10-

McGuinness, D. 1997. *Why Our Children Can't Read* NY: Free Press. Paperback: 1998. NY:Simon and Schuster

McGuinness, D. 2004. *Growing a Reader From Birth*. NY: W.W. Norton.

McGuinness, D. 2004. *Early Reading Instruction*. Boston: MIT Press

McGuinness, D. 2005. *Language Development and Learning to Read*. Boston: MIT Press.

Rice M. L. and Woodsmall, L. (1988). Lessons from television. Children's word learning when viewing. Child Development, 59, 420-429.

Printed in the United States
by Baker & Taylor Publisher Services